More Than Sunday School

EVANGELICAL TRAINING ASSOCIATION
110 Bridge Street • Box 327
Wheaton, Illinois 60189

Formally titled *More Than Sunday School: Fulfilling Church Objectives Through Educational Ministries.*

Unless otherwise noted, Scripture quotations are from the New American Standard Bible, © The Lockman Foundation 1960, 1962, 1963, 1971, 1972, 1973, 1975, and is used by permission.

7 6 5 4
0 9 8 7 6

ISBN: 0-910566-55-0

CONTENTS

INTRODUCTION

Church education ministry has many forms of expression. All are best carried out by prepared and dedicated followers of Christ. Educational ministries reach into every aspect of church life and contribute to the cause of Christ and the spiritual growth of individuals. Through church education believers are prepared for ministry and doors of service are opened.

Although this current edition has been completely revised and updated by the Association editorial staff, it still reflects the substance of the original content which was the work of such noteworthy Christian educators as: J. Omar Brubaker, M.A.; Linda Cannell, Ed.D.; Eleanor Daniel, Ph.D.; Kenneth O. Gangel, Ph.D.; Edward L. Hayes, Ph.D.; Gilbert A. Peterson, Ed.D.; and others.

Each writer of this practical overview of current church educational ministries is an experienced Christian educator. Each is well qualified in the subject he/she presents and has served on the faculty of an ETA member school.

The book has been prepared for use as the text for an ETA Church Ministries Certificate course. It makes an excellent study guide for Christian education board members since each chapter is a separate topic and can be discussed independently. It is also a good text for schools offering a basic introductory course in the local church educational ministry.

As a Christian education resource or a survey of the potential educational outreach of a church, this book would be profitable for anyone interested in communicating biblical truth.

CHURCH EDUCATION

1

Church education is essential to the effectiveness of the local church. New and challenging educational ministries, as well as established programs, lead the church toward enlarged gospel witness. In this day of increased secular influence, economic fluctuations, and technological advancement, teaching God's truth should be a high priority in every church.

The broader term, Christian education, refers to various forms of educational institutions including Christian colleges, seminaries, and the exploding Christian day school movement. Many educators today prefer the term church education to describe the nurturing ministry of a local congregation.

The church's teaching ministry is not new; but has been at the center of Christianity from the beginning of New Testament days. Christ's commission of His disciples in Matthew 28 was to a teaching ministry and it found expression in the writings and practices of the early church. During the dark periods of the Middle Ages, it provided hope and later, educational emphasis dominated the Protestant Reformation.

In early America all education was Christian. Gradually, however, Christian influences in America decreased until today a spirit of secularism dominates the public schools and too few homes have family reading and study of God's Word.

The public school can no longer give religious education and only a minority of children from Christian families can attend Christian elementary and secondary schools. The church, therefore, must shoulder the task of preparing parents for Christian nurture at home and supplementing their efforts in vital and vibrant educational ministries as a part of church life.

What is church education?
Church education is the communication of the gospel through formal and informal educational programs so that the facts of Scripture are

presented clearly and individuals respond by personal faith in Christ and growth toward spiritual maturity.

Education requires the discipline of mind or character through study or instruction. Christian education is even more definitive, adding the spiritual and supernatural dimensions to the already dynamic process.

One educator defines Christian education as a process by which persons are confronted with and controlled by the Christian gospel. Christian education, as it functions within the local church, is an equipping ministry to all age levels that nurtures spiritual growth and outreach to the world.

Benefits of church education

A church that seriously considers the values of educational ministries should be convinced of how necessary church education is to fulfilling the church's mission.

Honors Christ's command

The church must teach, for Christ said, "Go therefore and make disciples of all nations...teaching them to observe all that I commanded you..." (Matt. 28:19,20). Throughout His earthly ministry Jesus was the outstanding example of a teacher. The apostles, as clearly shown in the book of Acts and the other New Testament writings, followed Christ's command and example. Education is still our challenge and the entire church is responsible for Christian nurture, not just those who actually perform classroom duties.

Provides evangelistic outreach

A biblical perspective of church education includes the full message of the gospel. At the heart of this message is the call to personal faith in Jesus Christ. Every church educational effort, according to the Word of God, involves the message of salvation. Luke points out that the disciples "kept right on teaching and preaching Jesus as the Christ" (Acts 5:42). The church must use every opportunity to present Christ through both traditional programs, such as Sunday school, summer Bible ministries, children's and youth clubs, and also through more contemporary community evangelism outreaches such as home Bible studies, after school and day camp ministries, and outreach efforts to groups sharing common situations in life.

Strengthens the believers

The central concern of church education is the spiritual growth of the believer—whether child, youth, or adult. A biblical church education ministry offers opportunities for growth through varied means, all focusing on explaining and applying God's Word.

Various age-level ministries, special interest groups, youth groups, and children's churches all provide special means for spiritual development.

Builds the church and its leadership

Adults are the vital ingredient in any sound plan of church education. Many adult Christians in the church learned to consider biblical truths during their childhood and adolescence. The church has previously built upon the estimate that three out of four people who become Christians are converted before they leave their teens. Also, most who enter vocational Christian service respond during those key years of decision. The mandate is not only to "save from," but also to "send out" (Matt. 9:37,38). Church education develops Christian disciples. Church education develops lay leadership. It is central to the purpose of the local church.

Establishes church's beliefs and practices

Important objectives of church education are that believers understand the church's basic beliefs and that they can intelligently explain why they are Christians. Many believers, however, become perplexed when witnessing to others or discussing their faith. They discover that many of their convictions were simply accepted without really understanding their meanings and implications.

Believers also need to understand the significance of the church's activities and practices. Why is an offering taken? What do the bread and cup mean in the communion service? What is the significance of baptism? Why do we sing hymns and what do they mean? Explaining these essential aspects of meaningful church participation represent a challenge for the teaching ministry.

Gives parental guidance

Adults need spiritual guidance and wisdom if they are to obey the injunction of Scripture to bring up their children "in the nurture and admonition of the Lord." An effective church education ministry provides opportunities for parents to grow in their ability to establish and maintain effective teaching at home. The key educational agency is the family and it needs all the support a local church can provide.

Conserves church heritage

The Christian church has a rich heritage of God at work in the lives of men and women. The biblical record of both the Old and New Testaments, as well as church history in general, tells of spiritual awakenings and victories that accompanied studying and applying the Scriptures. This heritage serves to remind and encourage church educators to communicate both the Scriptures and the accounts of how God has worked in His church down through the ages.

Relationship to other church ministries

Educational ministries are not only valuable on their own but also relate closely to other areas of church ministry.

To preaching

Since much teaching takes place in effective preaching, the church's educational ministry is closely related to its pulpit ministry. Both preaching and teaching have a theological foundation, so it is essential that the theology presented from the pulpit is taught in the classroom. One author compares teaching to the Mississippi River, noting that it is a mighty river rather than a collection of puddles, swamps, and meandering streams because all its tributaries flow eventually and entirely into the main stream. Preaching and teaching have a common purpose that builds the main stream of church life.

To administration

Church education is an integral part of the total church ministry. Therefore, definite lines of administrative relationship need to be established. This begins with recognizing the central place of the pastor as minister of the entire congregation. When the church adds a minister or director of Christian education to its staff, specified areas of responsibility are assigned. A clear understanding should also be established as to authority, procedures, and personal relationships among all staff personnel.

The committee or board of Christian education, discussed in the final chapter of this text, is usually responsible for interrelating and correlating the total church program with regard to church education.

Organization of church education

The four factors that contribute to successfully organizing church education include the personnel involved in the program, the program itself, the facilities and equipment available, and the finances needed to carry out the program.

Personnel

Although church education is related to every member of the congregation, specified leadership is needed to organize, correlate, and give direction. Enlisting and training leaders for the various ministries is a large and continuing task. This task, however, is greatly assisted by planning a continuous leadership development program which includes foundational courses in Bible and Christian education. Churches which offer this type training usually accomplish their leadership goals.

Program

Success of any church educational program can be evaluated by whether or not aims are stated clearly and are attainable. The scope of the program should cover needed content areas and enough time must be allotted to teach this content.

Aims give direction, provide a basis for selecting materials and activities, assure clear presentation of lessons, provide continuity, and give a basis for measurement. Aims have an essential place in the entire educational program.

Three major areas of aims are prominent in church education: evangelism, edification, and equipping for service.

• *Evangelism*, the placing of personal faith in Christ, is a basic. Understanding the gospel is, of course, involved. In this context, each educational effort of the church is in itself a vital force for evangelism and what is today called pre-evangelism. Many times adult conversions can be traced to teaching given in earlier years.

• *Edifying*, the process of bringing the believer into spiritual maturity, is also at the heart of church education (Eph. 4:11-16). It associates application with knowledge. Thus, edification, especially in terms of Christian behavior, becomes an important measure of the success of church educational efforts.

• *Equipping*, the means of spiritual maturity and ministry opportunity, must be provided. Any effective educational program includes these opportunities at various levels and for believers of all ages.

The scope of educational programs in the local church has traditionally included the pulpit and the Sunday school class. Added to these important foundations, however, are newer, very significant ministries. Among these are: summer Bible ministry which could add many hours of instruction; weekday youth and children's activities which provide further outreach; and retreats and camping programs which broaden the educational program into an entirely different teaching dimension.

The increased teaching time in a comprehensive program is important. Just as important, however, are the increased opportunities to reach individuals on a variety of age levels and areas of personal interest.

Finance

Educational ministry should always be an important, and early, part of budget planning if the biblical mandate is taken seriously. Each local church should be careful to make adequate provision for each ministry so that it is able to carry on its work as effectively as possible. When the church has a board or committee of Christian education, one of its responsibilities is preparing and using such a budget.

Equipment and facilities

The church supports its teachers and workers in their educational effort with adequate facilities and equipment. At the same time, the quality of facilities and equipment also shows its people a genuine concern for quality teaching. Carefully selected teaching resources, chairs and tables of proper height, chalkboards, and a church resources center for student and teacher use are valuable assets to the ministry of church education.

Summary

The local church is responsible for the Christian nurture of its people. This responsibility is both a challenge and privilege. The focus of church education, regardless of church size, centers on reaching individuals with the gospel and guiding them into Christian living. This involves children, youth, and adults in various aspects of church and home activities.

The relationship of the educational program to the total church ministry is one of unity and correlation. The theology of the classroom, for example, must be in keeping with the theology of the pulpit. Similarly, established lines of responsibility and close coordination are essential.

Effective church education must also have aims. These relate to evangelism, edification, and equipping for Christian service. In carrying out its educational aims, the alert church will use every means available to it, including the educational ministries described in this book.

Review and discussion questions

1. What distinguishes church education from education in general?
2. Why is it important for the church to have an educational ministry?
3. What was Christ's attitude toward teaching?
4. Examine several instances in the New Testament where Christ is teaching or is referred to as a teacher and discuss His methods of teaching.
5. Compare the teaching emphasis of Christ and Paul using specific New Testament references.
6. What is the relationship of church education to the total congregational ministry?
7. What are the basic objectives of church education?
8. Prepare a list of church educational objectives and discuss how a particular church educational ministry, other than the Sunday school, might meet those objectives.
9. What is the place of educational ministries in a total church ministry?
10. Describe the teaching ministry of the early church using Matthew 28:16-20, Acts 2:42-47, and Ephesians 4:11-16.

Application activities

1. List all the organizations in your church involved in church education and chart their relationships to each other.
2. Collect examples of Christian influence (or lack of it) from current newspapers and magazines and relate your findings to church education.
3. Prepare a list of church educational objectives for your congregation, basing it on the specific needs of your church and those in your community.

CHURCH AND HOME

2

Church-home cooperation is essential to the church's education ministry. God charged both the church and the home with the responsibility of Christian education. In the Old Testament, the home was the basic educational agency for Jewish society (Deut. 6:4-10). The apostle Paul reflected this in New Testament teaching as he wrote: "And, fathers, do not provoke your children to anger; but bring them up in the discipline and instruction of the Lord" (Eph. 6:4). Home instruction, however, has not precluded the need for faithful volunteers to teach God's truth within the church's educational program.

Realizing that the family and the church have a joint ministry, in today's society where the family has become so fragmented, this challenge becomes ever more important and, in many situations, increasingly more difficult.

With the ever-increasing incidence of divorce, unmarried people adopting or bearing children, marriage not always being a primary goal of young people, single parent homes, remarriages and blended families, even defining what is meant by the term *family* is more difficult. Although many would like to believe these changing "family" situations occur only outside the church, in reality, it is becoming more and more prevalent among church members and attenders. Nevertheless it is only as the church and home cooperate enthusiastically that Christian education can be fully effective. In order for the church and home to cooperate, in today's setting, changes and adaptations often need to be made to accomplish this goal.

What is church-home educational cooperation?

Church-home educational cooperation is a planned program where the church assists and supports the home in communicating spiritual truth to the whole family by teaching and by example.

Benefits of church-home cooperation

When the church and home cooperate, both benefit. The home strengthens the church's ministry by broadening its base of operation and by reinforcing its teaching in the home. And homes are helped when the church recognizes the importance of the home and helps families utilize the church's resources.

The basic focus of both the church and the home is the individual believer who benefits directly as the home models and encourages church teaching.

Types of church-home cooperation

The cooperation needed between the church and the home should flow in both directions.

The church assisting the home

The church works with the home by strengthening the spiritual life of family members, providing information and courses, and demonstrating patterns for Christian living.

The church and home may be separate teaching agencies; but the persons taught and the teaching responsibility are held in common. The church's activities strongly influence the spiritual atmosphere of the home and family fellowship. Family devotions, for example, can be greatly strengthened by the church's teaching and encouragement.

The church that provides specialized information and spiritual counsel serves as a resource guide for parents and other guardians. Such information or questions may pertain to the meaning of Scripture, church and denominational history and practice, or the application of Christian ideals to behavior and service.

Christian parents and other guardians are sometimes poorly prepared to answer perplexing family questions. Many homes, therefore, reflect the pattern of their surrounding society, rather than Christian standards. Here, alert church-home cooperation can offer parents a practical resource for sound biblical guidance.

Paul enjoined: "Be of the same mind toward one another" (Rom. 12:16a). The church is a community under the law of God and alive by the Spirit of God. Love is to control its ministry, teaching its members how to relate to fellow believers. Persons are to be accepted, encouraged, and committed to God in prayer. Barriers which separate are thus broken down in Christ. This kind of church is a pattern for home life as Christian principles of human relationships are put into practice.

Families which experience crucial life events such as marriage, birth of children, dedication and baptism, choice of vocation, divorce and perhaps remarriage, serious illness, retirement, and death also require the help of the local church in the form of encouragement, support, and counsel.

The home assisting the church

The work of the church needs home support. A local church is only as strong as the families which make up its ranks. Through its individual members, the family strengthens the church by sharing teaching and leadership responsibilities. As a unit, it helps the church be the biblical "family of families."

Through the enthusiastic cooperation and support of church educational ministries, the home both strengthens and encourages the congregation. Parents helping children with Sunday school lessons, supporting standards of childhood and adolescent behavior, providing transportation and refreshments, assisting and teaching classes, and just being interested in activities are practical evidences of support.

Parents' attitudes toward the church and Christian living, as well as their own practical examples, greatly influence the rest of the family.

Finally, the home supports the church program through regular giving and by projects undertaken as a family (or in conjunction with other church families). Voluntary service performed by families often makes it possible to carry out ministries which might otherwise be neglected.

Relationship to other church ministries

The home includes all age groups and touches each educational program. Church-home cooperation, therefore, should be evidenced in and through each organization and the church will be wise to make every possible provision to draw the home into its planning and programming.

Sunday school and the home are best able to cooperate when the daily impact in the home supports and furthers the weekly Sunday school lesson. This is accomplished by close communication between the home and the Sunday school. Many Sunday school curriculum publishers seek to integrate home Bible instruction with the Sunday school teaching through unifying the Bible lesson themes or portions of Scripture studied for both parents' and children's classes.

An alert local church today is aware of the breakdown of many families. Without diluting its emphasis on the family unit and alternate "family" settings, it will seek creative ways to minister to single, divorced, widowed, and separated parents as well as adults who are not part of a family. Such a broad ministry will also consider a growing group of very important church members —the older adult.

Organizing for church-home cooperation

To understand how a local church can organize for proper church-home cooperation, personnel, program, and financing need to be considered.

Personnel

In addition to the overall supervision of pastor, Christian education director, and board of Christian education, a parent-staff fellowship or a church-home committee can be helpful. These committee members are usually representative of those parents and other interested adults whose family members are involved in the church's educational ministries. In some instances a separate subcommittee of the board of Christian education may serve in this capacity.

Some churches are now adding to their staffs ministers of family life whose central responsibility focuses on developing family nurture. These staff members might be volunteers or full or part-time professionals. Their responsibilities include such areas as teaching and counseling those preparing for marriage and parenting, as well as marriage enrichment and remedial family intervention.

Program

The means by which the church and home work together may be grouped in three ways: the church going to the home, the home coming to the church, and the church and home going to the community.

The church going to the home As church leadership visits in homes of church members, rapport is established. Purpose for home visits are:
- Gaining knowledge of student's home environment
- Establishing a relationship between church and home
- Determining evangelistic needs
- Securing home cooperation in teaching ministry
- Sharing gospel witness and pertinent literature
- Evaluating interest in ministry opportunities
- Communicating availability for counseling
- Determining the needs for and interest in classes which address family issues

The church also may periodically have contact with homes through a parents' bulletin or magazine. These publications might provide information about the various educational programs in which family members participate, help for building Christian homes, guidance and curriculum suggestions for family devotions, and Bible instruction. Care and attention should be given to be sure that these publications do not assume the family structure includes a mother, a father, and one or more children living together.

Also, appropriate church library books and video and audio cassette tapes may be taken to homes for extension ministry.

The home coming to the church As families become involved in church activities other than the Sunday worship services, the opportunities to assist them expand. There must be, however, a wise balance between church and home activity and care exercised to keep the good from hindering the best. Churches must resist the temptation to over-program. In their zeal to provide every opportunity for nurture and service, some churches may actually contribute to family break-up by taking one or more family members out of the home to attend or serve in their educational ministries. To try to counteract this problem, churches usually seek to schedule most of the weekday activities on one or at most two nights to avoid competing with family life.

Class curriculum and instruction especially geared to home interests, such as family devotions and parenting Christian children, may serve well in helping to establish and strengthen Christian homes. This may include adult elective Sunday school courses or home Bible study groups which provide both fellowship and learning. Social programs arranged at regular intervals may encourage involvement by entire families and can be valuable learning experiences as well.

Periodic open house programs for parents and family groups create lasting impressions. Departmental family nights or visitation Sundays are helpful as well.

Parents and other guardians who accept teaching or leadership positions within the church find this spiritual challenge carrying over into family matters. Others may assist as departmental or class parents with responsibility for communicating with students' parents and encouraging parental projects.

Every family member cannot be part of every church activity. It is important, however, for every family member whenever possible to have a part in some church activity and for churches and families to work together in community outreach.

Church and home going to the community Church-sponsored home Bible studies, cooperative programs relating to marriage and family issues, and community visitation programs offer vital Christian contacts with the community. Outreach can also be accomplished with family suppers and social evenings to which community people can be invited and where they will meet Christian families.

A church open house may provide an excellent opportunity for the community to learn about the church's mission and which of the neighbors attend and serve there.

Friendship evangelism, a program which Christian families invite unchurched families to their homes and share their gospel witness, has also proven effective in many churches.

Financing

Financing for church-home cooperative programs is usually part of the regular church budget. This includes provision for devotional material or other literature for the home and possibly assisting needy families in times of economic stress.

Summary

Church-home cooperation is essential to an effective church education program. Both the church and the family members benefit by working closely together. The church serves as a resource guide for parents and other guardians, offering specialized information and counsel. The home reinforces the church's educational ministry both by its Christian witness and by its share in the educational leadership.

Beside the regular worship service and other weekly activities, the church ministers to the home through visitation, literature, and purposeful social activities.

The church and home also share in community outreach through home Bible studies, social activities, community visitation, and open house programs.

Parent-staff fellowship or a church-home committee related to the board of Christian education strengthens the organization of church-home cooperation.

Review and discussion questions

1. What role does the home play in the church's educational program?
2. Name some early experiences that influenced your attitude toward the gospel and how effective church-home cooperation might have assured more positive results.
3. In what ways does the church strengthen the home?
4. How might young peoples' Christian development suffer were they to have no church, but have to depend wholly on the instruction given in the home?
5. In what areas can the church provide specific help to parents?
6. What type ministry does church-home cooperation require?
7. How do church and home responsibilities sometimes make conflicting demands and how this might be avoided?

Application activities

1. List the major areas of Christian life in which Christian young people should receive instruction. After each subject, indicate the agency (church, home, school, or other) which should take the major responsibility and how other agencies might cooperate.
2. Analyze a Christian periodical in terms of its help to each member of your family. For this purpose, you may wish to proceed by listing the names of the family members, those articles pertinent to each, and the values of the information presented.
3. Outline a program for promoting Christian education in the family. List ways for your Sunday school and other church educational ministries to better communicate and cooperate with the home.

4. Realizing the diversity of many home situations today, make a list of ways your church educational program has changed to both accommodate and minister to all families.

SUNDAY SCHOOL

3

Both as an effective evangelistic force and a program for teaching the Bible, God has blessed the Sunday school for over two centuries.

What is the Sunday school?
The Sunday school is a church-sponsored educational agency which functions on Sunday and provides a curriculum of Bible study and evangelistic emphasis for all ages.

Although there were antecedents as far back as Old Testament times, the Sunday school movement had its beginning in Gloucester, England, in the year 1780. Robert Raikes' purpose in beginning schools on Sunday was to teach children of slum areas to read and write, using the Bible as a text.

The movement developed slowly and Raikes was severely criticized for "desecrating the Sabbath Day." Early supporters included William Fox, founder of the first Sunday school society in England, and John and Charles Wesley. At the time of Raikes' death in 1811 thousands of Sunday schools had been started in England and the movement was firmly established.

The Sunday school in America began in 1785 and played an important role in shaping the national life of the country, especially in the developing frontier. As the Bible was gradually moved out of its original place in public schools, the great task of teaching God's Word fell largely upon the Sunday school.

Benefits of the Sunday school

Both Old and New Testaments stress teaching. God commanded Moses to "assemble the people, men, and women, and children...that they may hear and learn and...observe all the words of this law" (Deut. 31:12). Parents are exhorted to bring up their children "in the nurture and admonition of the Lord" (Eph. 6:4

19

KJV). Christ, the master teacher, conducted a traveling school in which he taught a group of twelve disciples. The modern Sunday school carries on this teaching emphasis.

Provides systematic Bible teaching

In most churches, the Sunday school is prominent in providing systematic teaching of the Word of God and its application in Christian life and service. It offers many advantages: continuity, lay instruction, a ministry to all ages, and a regular time and place of meeting.

Presents claims of Christ

The evangelical Sunday school confronts modern man with the message of salvation. It stands at the forefront of evangelism in American history; and continues to offer the church one of its most potent outreaches. The great evangelist Dwight L. Moody noted this, championing the cause of the Sunday school in the nineteenth century.

Gives opportunity for service

Because it ministers to more people, the Sunday school provides more opportunities for Christian service than any other agency in the church. In addition to teachers, Sunday schools need secretaries, pianists, and people with a wide range of other interests and abilities. With limited formal training, a lay person willing to prepare and serve can find a place of useful ministry.

Promotes church growth

At the end of the 20th century, the Sunday school still promotes church growth and fruitfulness. It not only adds members to the body of Christ and to the local church; but also provides a training ground for the preparation of leaders in other church ministries. The Sunday school is indeed, as Clarence H. Benson said, "the gold mine of the church."

Builds character

The Sunday school strengthens moral character. It deters crime. Its influence on moral standards has been far-reaching and it continues as a vital force in the building of Christian citizenship.

Types of Sunday school organization

As with many organizations, Sunday schools vary in length, time of meeting, and in how they are divided.

Variations in length

Today's Sunday schools take a variety of forms. Most meet for an hour before or after morning worship service; but some extend children's Sunday school session through church time. Such sessions can include class lessons, discussion, worship, and some play or learning activity.

Variations in time of meeting

In addition to the possibility of meeting before or after the worship service, classes can be held between two worship services, concurrently during two worship services, or in the afternoon. Many urban churches are using their facilities in the afternoon for minority or foreign language Sunday schools.

Variations in divisions

One simple division in the Sunday school is by school grade. Smaller churches usually prefer departments composed of one, two, or three grades depending upon the size of the school. The grading or departmentalization, however, will usually be decided by size, choice of curriculum, or availability and flexibility of facilities.

Although opinions vary, most churches feel that to provide the personal attention children require, their classes should be less than 10 students each, while youth and adult classes might number up to 20-30.

Relationship to other church ministries

In the ever-expanding educational outreach of the church, new Christian education ministries continually emerge. Traditional or contemporary, each must have a clearly defined purpose and position. While the Sunday school is usually the major teaching program of the church, boys' and girls' clubs and youth programs are important too, and must be carefully coordinated into the total program by the board of Christian education.

Organization of the Sunday school

Organization in the Sunday school has to do with personnel, curriculum, and instruction. Administration includes recruiting, training, and supervising the people who perform the work outlined in the planning. Efficient organization unifies a Sunday school, clarifies responsibility, and seeks to implement the objectives of church education.

Personnel

Since the success of the Sunday school depends so largely on the Christian personality and dynamic of the leadership, loyal and energetic people are needed to assume the tasks with determination and devotion.

Unless the church is of sufficient size to employ a minister or director of Christian education, the *pastor* carries a key responsibility for the program of Christian education. Working closely with the Sunday school superintendent, a concerned pastor inspires, energizes, and counsels the Sunday school staff. Regardless of whether the church staff includes a minister or director of Christian education, the pastor should take the lead in making Sunday school a vital means of furthering the mission and ministry of the church.

The supervision of the Sunday school requires educational vision, administrative ability, and untiring effort. The effective *Sunday school superintendent* believes in the Sunday school, works well with the staff, and is genuinely concerned for the spiritual growth of every student. The superintendent serves with the same compassionate concern as the pastor for the spiritual growth of those under his/her care.

Recruiting teachers and other staff is a major task of the Sunday school superintendent. When recruiting, the superintendent needs to stress the importance of the job, fulfilling the job description and standards, and serving for a specific time period. Superintendents who emphasize the positive aspects of ministry in the Sunday school make recruiting easier.

The *department superintendent* serves in much the same capacity as the Sunday school superintendent; but is responsible for the work of only one department and reports to the superintendent.

The *Sunday school secretary* renders important service to Christ and the Sunday school by recording accurately the minutes of the staff meeting, handling correspondence promptly, and keeping meaningful statistics.

The *treasurer* performs a task that requires honesty, accuracy, and promptness. Monetary gifts to God should be handled properly.

Other members of the staff, such as *departmental secretaries, music director,* and *media center director,* are appointed as needs arise. These staff members interrelate in the properly functioning organizational design.

Ultimately, the success of a Sunday school depends upon the teachers. It is imperative, therefore, that the right persons be appointed to lead the classes.

Teachers shoulder enormous responsibility to maintain right personal relationship with God, to learn all they can about the students they teach, and to study earnestly the Word of God and the best methods of teaching. Teaching time in Sunday school is short and should be used to eternal advantage, constantly depending on the Holy Spirit as the source of strength.

Many churches use a structure similar to the diagram at the top of the next page.

Program

Though the Sunday school is responsible for teaching the Word of God, it must also provide for teacher training, instruction in worship, evangelism, and mission education. Often these fit naturally into the regular curriculum of the school.

Those responsible for choosing Sunday school curriculum must make their selections carefully. It is important that the curriculum

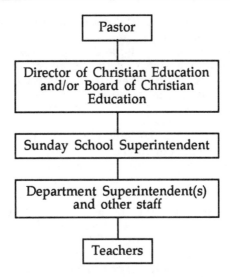

be correlated between age levels. Since almost all curriculum publishers provide some method for unifying instruction, most Sunday schools use one curriculum publisher's materials throughout the program.

When selecting Sunday school curriculum consider some very important questions.

- Are the materials theologically sound?
- Do the lessons encourage personal Bible study?
- Do they provide sufficient help for the teacher?
- Are the materials attractive?

As stated earlier, an important aim of the Sunday school is evangelism. To best accomplish this aim teachers should know each student's personal relationship to Christ and teach with individual spiritual needs in mind. Training in evangelism should be included in preparing Sunday school leaders.

Most Sunday school teachers are not professionally trained for their classroom duties. Leadership preparation, therefore, is essential and cannot be neglected.

Training can include formal teacher training classes, seminars, and instruction during full staff or departmental meetings. Teachers may gain further training through reading books about effective teaching, one-on-one coaching, and attending Christian education conferences and conventions.

Facilities and equipment

Trained staff members need adequate facilities and equipment to be fully effective. Classrooms are teachers' workshops and equipment their tools. Space needs should allow for worship, teaching, learning activities, and social activities. Minimum standards require that classrooms be clean and light, attractively decorated, and large enough and adapted to comfortable learning. Essential items of equipment include suitable chairs, tables of the right shape and heights, and supply closets. Chalkboards and bulletin boards are also on the list of essentials, as well as tuned pianos, play equipment for preschool children, and conveniently located toilet facilities.

Financing

Churches that include the Sunday school in the church budget should be sure sufficient finances are provided to carry out all aspects of the Sunday school's educational program.

Summary

The Sunday school has come a long way since 1780. It has developed into the church's leading educational ministry, providing opportunity for systematic Bible study for all ages, as well as offering a vital means for evangelistic outreach.

Because it is essentially a lay movement, the work depends largely upon local church leadership preparation to help teachers and other staff members provide effective teaching. Even after more than two hundred years, the Sunday school still offers the largest opportunity of any church ministry for Christians to use their gifts in the Lord's service.

Review and discussion questions

1. What is the distinctive purpose of the Sunday school?
2. How did the Sunday school originate?
3. What is the biblical basis for the Sunday school?
4. Outline the present grouping of students in your Sunday school and evaluate its effectiveness.
5. What is meant by the statement that the teacher is the key to a successful Sunday school?
6. What training opportunities should be available to Sunday school staff?
7. Discuss the place of evangelism as it relates to each division of the Sunday school.
8. What are some criteria that could guide church leaders in selecting teaching materials for the Sunday school?

Application activities

1. Prepare a detailed job description for the superintendent in a Sunday school of two hundred people.
2. Make a chart of all the classes of your Sunday school, indicating how you would handle a fifty percent increase in attendance.
3. Visit all the classrooms in your Sunday school facilities. Make a list of ways their appearance and effectiveness can be improved at minimum cost.

Major curriculum publishers

Many denominations publish or imprint their own curriculum materials and we encourage you to investigate and become thoroughly familiar with all denominational materials. Several interdenominational publishing companies, however, service thousands of churches with different types of evangelical Sunday school curriculum. Addresses for some of these companies are listed below.

Augsburg Fortress
426 S. 5th St. Box 1209
Minneapolis, MN 55440

Concordia Publishing House
3558 S. Jefferson
St. Louis, MO 63118

David C. Cook Publishing
4050 Lee Vance View
Colorado Springs, CO 80918

Gospel Light Publishing Co.
2300 Knoll Ave.
Ventura, CA 93003

National Baptist Publishing
7145 Centennial Blvd.
Nashville, TN 37209

Scripture Press Publications
PO Box 36640
Colorado Springs, CO 80936-6640

Standard Publishing
8121 Hamilton Ave.
Cincinnati, OH 45231

Union Gospel Press
P.O. Box 6059
Cleveland, OH 44101

Urban Ministries
1350 W. 103rd St.
Chicago, IL 60643

HOME BIBLE STUDIES

4

A very effective way for people to study the Bible together is the home Bible study. Unlike the Sunday school class, which uses the local church as a place of contact to learn God's truth, the home Bible study utilizes a home-oriented approach. Those sponsoring the study invite neighbors and friends into family rooms and living rooms for an informal and inductive look into God's Word.

What are church-sponsored home Bible studies?
Church-related Bible study programs meet in homes, at daytime or evening hours, with an emphasis on informal atmosphere and a balance of personal sharing and serious inductive study.

God has placed in each heart the desire for relationship and belonging. Small group study and discussion of God's revelation has always been a key factor in fulfilling these needs. The Old Testament patriarchal family was the first model which later produced the New Testament church pattern.

The New Testament pattern, seen in Acts 2:42,46; 5:42; 18:7; Romans 16:5; 1 Corinthians 16:19; and Colossians 4:15 envisioned a small group which met to share, learn, teach, and encourage each other. This small group approach characterized the church for the first 200 years.

Early church history reflected a similar small group pattern. The Waldensians, Anabaptists, Pietists, Moravians, and Wesleyan groups followed such a model. Currently, groups such as Inter-Varsity, Campus Crusade, and Navigators also utilize small group Bible study as their primary ministry tool.

In many areas of the world, the greatest evangelism and growth of new believers is still emerging from small group Bible studies.

Benefits of home Bible studies

This important educational ministry contributes heavily to the church's better meeting personal needs, providing a setting for acceptance and care, creating a platform for evangelism, discipling, gift discerning, and ministry equipping, modeling biblical family values, and providing a basis for individual ministry to the world.

Better meets personal needs

In the small group environment, the personal needs of the participants are more readily recognized and met. Societal stresses promote loneliness and insensitivity, but small group settings promote individuality and relationship.

Provides a setting for acceptance and care

As the local church grows larger, people report increased estrangement and a sense of decreased care. The small group, however, can provide an "island" of personal acceptance and care that neither society or the large church provides.

Creates a platform for ministry

Home Bible studies are frequently used quite successfully as an evangelistic technique; but are also effective in producing discipling, the discovery of spiritual gifts, and equipping and training to implement these gifts and their call to minister.

Models biblical family values

The breakdown of the family and its biblical values is one of the most serious problems facing society today. The small group Bible study models those biblical values that clarify and encourage proper relationships between men and women, racial diversity, and generational and cultural differences.

Provides a basis for individual ministry

Most believers are searching for avenues of ministry which are meaningful and fulfilling to them. Not only does the home Bible study provide ministry opportunities within its structure (leader, teacher, host, recruiter, etc.) but the close interaction between participants often generate fresh new opportunities for ministry, either to those persons or referrals beyond the group.

Many churches have discovered that home Bible studies have been their greatest source of new inquirers and members. At one time this was true of the Sunday school and in some places it still is. God is reawakening the church, however, to its early history of using small group Bible study to bring people into contact with God's Word so they may be born again and made a part of the body of Christ. Even believers in search of a new church home often make their first contact through a Bible study.

Types of home Bible studies

Seven types of home Bible studies can be identified in many churches, although often any specific program would most likely include a combination of these seven.

Contact

The purpose of this category is to generate contact with non-believers. Usually quite informal, the approach is to allow unbelievers to feel non-threatened in the group. Often there are only a few believers in the group. The approach to Bible study is personal discovery of Bible truth that is relevant to the unbeliever's world.

Evangelism

In this type, the purpose is more than contact. It is exploring the claims of Christ upon the person. Sometimes such groups evolve into nurture and growth groups, while other groups hand off their members to such groups after they profess faith.

Nurture

Building faith upon the gospel acceptance is the purpose of this type. Its goal, however, is limited to basic nurture in the faith. Groups of this kind are composed of believers, though some are more mature, using the group experiences as a ministry to new believers.

Growth

Spiritual maturity beyond nurture is the purpose of this type. Since issues are highly life-related, the Bible study areas are quite topical. Mutual self-discovery of God's design for life is the theme.

Support

Groups which share common lifestyles or problems (single, divorced, drug or alcohol addicted, handicapped, seniors, etc.) use this common denominator as a catalyst for studying the Bible as it relates to this experience.

Service

Somewhat similar to a support group, these groups center around a ministry cause (retirement homes, prisons, backyard clubs, music groups, etc.) as the means for their Bible study.

Satellite

Many of the mega-churches have developed this type of home Bible study to be a mini-church experience. With a format of unique worship, fellowship, and edification, this group purposes to provide a Sunday church experience on a weekday or night in microcosm.

Relationship to other educational ministries

The relationship of home Bible studies to the local church is often widely debated. Some have suggested that if the studies relate too closely to the church, some people will not come or free discussion will be hampered by the church's creed and practices. But all forms of Christian ministry only gain their validity by their commitment and ability to serve local churches.

As people trust Christ in the home Bible study, they need to attach themselves to a wider flock and have a shepherd lead them in the further nurturing process. An integral connection without absolute control seems to be the best relationship a church can sustain with its home Bible studies.

Developing home Bible studies

To learn how to develop and direct home Bible studies, the community setting, time and materials, learning approach, and home climate for Bible studies need to be considered.

Community setting

It is important to consider the economic level and cultural characteristics of the community where the Bible study is to be held. People in one income bracket, for example, tend to be able to draw other people of the same income level to a home Bible study. The geographical proximity of their homes will most likely be closer as well, and their interests and needs coincide more closely. This is, of course, true of the cultural characteristics as well. Though we want to be as broad as possible in our relationship experiences, successful home Bible studies are based on the compatibility of the participants.

Time and materials

Many home Bible studies meet for one or two hours a week at a time convenient for the participants. When the study meets for two hours a week, a common pattern is to run for a six-week period beginning in mid-September and concluding at the end of October. For those home Bible studies using ETA textbooks as their curriculum, this allows the group to complete one course in that time period. This two-hour per week model usually begins again in mid-January, concluding the end of February, beginning again in mid-March, concluding the end of April. This allows plenty of breaks in the scheduling of courses to accommodate busy adult lifestyles.

The one-hour per week format usually begins the first week of September and concludes the end of November, then begins again the first week of February and finishes at the end of April.

Of course, some home Bible studies meet all through the year. Since it is characteristic of adults to "drop-in" and "drop-out" in education, perpetual Bible studies must be prepared for considerable participant transience.

The ETA Certificate Program is a strong motivator for adult retention in either the six- or twelve-week model. ETA courses which are uniquely suited to home Bible studies are: *Growing Toward Spiritual Maturity, You and Your Bible, Biblical Beliefs, The Triune God, New Testament Survey, Understanding People,* and *Your Ministry of Evangelism.* Other courses often used are: *Effectively Leading, World Missions Today,* and *Understanding Teaching.*

Learning approach

Since adults have distinctive learning characteristics, home Bible studies must employ a learning approach which reflects these characteristics. Adult learners are self-directed, with a significant reservoir of life experiences which they want to interact with any new truth. Their social role strongly orients them to their learning readiness. And problem-solving is far more preferable to the adult than subject-centered learning.

The adult learner, therefore, expects to play a major role in the entire learning experience. This means the adult will expect to have decision-making input in curriculum selection, time and class location, teaching/guide selection, and the learning methodology.

Since many adult learning experiences have employed more traditional learning approaches like those used in teaching children (teacher active/learner passive), considerable effort must be made by home Bible study leaders to move more toward the adult learning approach (both teacher and learner active). Usually that takes four phases, which may take many months to complete. Phase one begins with the traditional teacher active/learner passive approach. Phase two sees the teacher heavily using participative teaching methods. By phase three, the teacher now serves only as guide to the group. Group members take on responsibility for class pre-study and preparation. By phase four, the teacher has become one of the participants. The group takes full responsibility for the learning experience.

The leader should maintain an open and pleasing personality, with disciplined attitudes and mannerisms so they do not adversely affect the group members.

The leader should be sure that everyone has a Bible. Differences in translations need not constitute a problem. Rather, when group members read from various Bible versions, they can better clarify some texts and their study will be enhanced.

Bible study leaders should constantly be developing and training other leaders. A time might arrive when leaders feel the need to start new Bible studies in other areas and necessarily leave their original groups on their own. No Bible study should become so bound to one leader that the group falls apart without that person. If proper growth and training have been taking place, someone will be prepared to lead at the appropriate time.

Future leaders can also be developed by having all group members share in leading the discussion from the very formative days of the group. In these situations, the regular leader should always be available to help avoid random discussions.

Home climate

Wisely selecting sites for home Bible studies contributes to their success. The hosts should be typical group members. This will eliminate social strain and promote free discussion.

The host's enthusiasm also helps. Meaningful response and continuing participation depends on the enthusiasm of everyone associated with the Bible study.

More often than not, the sessions will be held somewhere other than at the leader's home since both hosting and leading the Bible study could be an overload for one person or couple.

Bible studies should be enjoyable as well as educational. Keep the atmosphere friendly and informal and serve refreshments. Provide child care if mothers or couples with small children attend.

Participants in the evangelistic Bible study sometimes come from many church backgrounds. When these people trust Christ and begin to grow as Christian, they should depend upon the Holy Spirit to give them theological discernment and church direction. The home Bible study should never proselytize but rather seek to be a group that simply loves and studies the Bible.

Bible studies should not be allowed to become too small or too large. Less than five group members tends to be intimidating, and more than twenty will stifle effective discussions. Group members and leaders should not become disappointed when some people attend only one or two times and then drop out. A Bible study simply cannot reach everybody. It must concentrate on the people who continue to come and are interested in learning from God's Word.

Summary

Home Bible studies, having roots going back to New Testament times (Acts 2:46; 5:42), can be an effective means of propagating the gospel message, nurturing the new Christian, and edifying the believer.

Geographical locations, meeting times, size and makeup of the groups along with careful selection of leaders and the methods they use all contribute to the success of the program.

Group members' commitment to the local church is evidenced by inviting new converts to join a local body of believers, developing and training new leaders for future ministry, and fellowshiping among the believers.

Review and discussion questions

1. What types of home Bible studies are being used in Christian education?
2. What steps would you take to begin a home Bible study?
3. How does a church benefit from home Bible studies?
4. Discuss home Bible studies that are meeting in your community.
5. How does a church determine what type of home Bible studies to conduct?
6. How does a church administer a home Bible study teaching program?
7. What are the advantages and disadvantages of home Bible studies?
8. Discuss the values of church sponsorship of home Bible studies.

Application activities

1. Visit a home Bible study and prepare a report on your experience. Note location and size of class, materials used in addition to the Bible, teaching methods, and the group constituency.
2. Interview a leader in an active home Bible study to discover his/her insights on who is reached and the materials and methods used.
3. Outline a program of home Bible studies which would specialize in meeting the needs of special groups such as singles and/or senior citizens.

SUMMER BIBLE MINISTRIES

5

Summer is a prime time for quality Bible teaching. The opportunities are limited only by imagination, planning, and commitment. A more relaxed pace and casual, flexible schedule can be viewed as a bridge to influence otherwise unreachable members of your community. Not so long ago the only summer ministry conducted by most churches was one or two weeks of Vacation Bible School. But this has changed for many congregations who are intent on expanding their summer ministries in an effort to reach their friends and neighbors for the Lord.

The first summer Bible ministry was conducted in New York City in 1898 when Mrs. Eliza Hawes became concerned over the needs of slum children about whom the church seemed to care little. Her Everyday Bible School lasted for six weeks and included elements still found in many of today's summer Bible ministries: singing, Bible lessons, and crafts. By 1925, this program usually took the form of what is now known as Vacation Bible School and had become an accepted part of nearly every congregation's educational program.

Through the years, these Vacation Bible Schools have adapted to many structures, as the needs of the local church has changed. Some churches conduct programs that represent the same aims and formats as Vacation Bible School, only another title for the program may be used. Nevertheless these ministries have served as a vital part of many churches' outreach teaching ministry.

What are summer Bible ministries?

Summer Bible ministries are weekday programs of Bible study and related activities for all ages, conducted by the church during the summer months.

They are called *summer* Bible ministries because they are conducted primarily during the summer months.

They are called summer *Bible* ministries because their basic purpose is to teach the Word of God.

They are called summer Bible *ministries* in that they are conducted by the church and geared to help students accept Christ and grow in Him.

Types of summer Bible ministries

Although the possibilities are numerous, four types of summer Bible ministries are most prevalent in local church programs: vacation schools, backyard Bible ministries, day camps, and one-day-per-week sessions.

Vacation schools

The vacation months of the summer still produce many Vacation Bible Schools, as they are traditionally known. These programs are still a vital ministry, whether known as VBS, Summerfest, Family Camp, or other titles. Some churches prefer to conduct their program immediately after the regular school year is out in late May or early June. They contend that the children are still in the habit of attending school and therefore are more attentive and cooperative. This also makes it possible to have the program before it conflicts with other camps, family vacations, and other events of the summer.

Still other churches prefer a later summer date. Some choose July purposely because it is the middle month. Others prefer an August date just before children are scheduled to return to school. These groups suggest that children are by now tired of summer vacation and ready for more structured learning again.

VBS used to be strictly a daytime program. Probably the most popular time has been a morning program conducted for two to three hours per day. Sometimes the program was conducted for the same amount of time in the afternoon, especially in rural communities where the women had to prepare a noon meal and entire families were needed for activities on the farm.

Similar lifestyle concerns gave birth to the evening VBS. Evening schools have become so popular that it now rivals the morning programs. The evening VBS program has allowed extension of the teaching ministry to an entirely new clientele and has permitted more working adult and family emphasis.

Backyard Bible ministries

Many churches, especially those with a family-oriented evening VBS, have added backyard Bible ministries to their summer programming. Programs of this type have proven to be effective evangelistic tools. They also make it possible for a new congregation to have a summer Bible ministry in spite of its lack of facility. Often VBS curriculum will provide instructions for adapting the material to this setting.

To get started, church leadership finds one or several homes whose residents (usually members of the congregation) will host a backyard Bible ministry and serve as a contact person in their neighborhoods. The necessary space is a yard with water and toilet facilities nearby. A garage is helpful on raining days.

Groups should be limited to ten to fifteen participants per yard. Sometimes only one age level is scheduled in one yard if several homes in the same neighborhood are available.

Staffing is relatively simple for this venture. The critical selection is the teacher(s), although a recreation leader would be helpful as well. Similar to Vacation Bible School, the time schedule varies from one-and-one-half to three hours.

The backyard summer Bible ministry is an effective means of reaching the children in households who are not associated with the church and who may be reluctant to send their children to the church building. If this kind of program is followed up well, people can be reached for the Lord.

Day camp

Other churches have developed a variety of day camp programs for all ages. These are usually conducted at a farm, park, or camp. Day camp programs are often conducted from single days to five days in succession over a one to two week period. Larger churches with available personnel may opt to extend the day camp program over the entire summer.

The site is of major importance. It needs to be protected place where the planned program can be carried out without interruption. Water and rest rooms are essential for day camps. Day camps should be relatively close to the church building. Swimming facilities and hiking trails may also be desirable. Transportation should also be addressed.

Staff is critical, especially since the program is conducted for long periods of time. The teachers and recreation leaders must be carefully selected and trained.

One day per week

Still other congregations have developed a one-day-per-week program for various age groups. One church, for example, conducts a program for preschool children one day in the week, for elementary children another day, and for teens still another day. These are sometimes done during the day; but some choose to conduct them at night.

One-day-per-week programs may range from two hours to an entire day, with perhaps the most popular being a morning or an afternoon. These programs generally differ from VBS in that they include more emphasis on recreation, field trips, and films and less on missions and/or crafts.

Benefits of summer Bible ministries

Summer Bible ministries can benefit a church's educational program in a number of ways.

Increases the teaching time

A two to three hour summer Bible ministry program, conducted for five days, for example, provides as much actual teaching time as an entire quarter of Sunday school. Double that for a ten-day program. At a time when vacations take a larger than ever bite out of the summer season, these calculations reveal the promise of summer Bible ministries.

Provides an outreach to the community

Summer Bible ministries allow a church to penetrate a community in a way that is often impossible when only Sunday teaching programs are conducted. Many parents who would not make the effort to get their children to a church program are receptive to an invitation to a summer teaching ministry. It, after all, interferes minimally with the parent's schedule. Other people recognize the desirability of religious teaching for their children and see one of these programs as an appropriate place for it to be done. Whatever the initial interest or motivation on the parent's part, the challenge to the church is to seize the opportunity. A systematic follow-up effort can bring many of these people to the Lord.

Allows time to reinforce and deepen learning experiences

Summer Bible teaching programs enable a teacher to build upon an individual's previous learning experiences. The longer time segment devoted to one session also allows for more efficient learning. A variety of learning experiences—Bible stories, music, learning activities, crafts, even recreation, centered around a teaching theme—maximizes the learning experience.

Develops potential workers

Summer Bible teaching programs provide an ideal resource from which to recruit new workers into other teaching ministries in the church. It is a perfect time to let potential teachers and other staff members try teaching, for the commitment is short term on the part of both the workers and the church. A pleasant first experience will encourage volunteers to consider longer commitments in Sunday school, the youth program, or other church educational ministries.

Organizing summer Bible ministries

Successful summer Bible ministries have a plan and are developed around that plan. Following the suggestions below will help make your summer Bible ministry successful.

Establish goals

The first step in developing an effective summer program is to set goals that will guide its implementation. If the Christian education board bears final responsibility for the program, the members should determine the intended goals prior to recruiting the director. If a director for the program is selected without this information available, the first task should be to state the goals.

Every summer Bible ministry should accomplish something— not merely be done just because it has always been. Determine the major emphasis to be accomplished. Obviously, Bible teaching is a major goal. But what about evangelism: Should students come only from your church or should other churches in the community be invited to participate? Will there be a major missions emphasis? What are the numerical goals, both in enrollment and outreach? How many new recruits should be added to the teaching corps? Stating the goals clearly and measurably will assist in further planning.

Choose dates and times

The first order of business is for the supervisory group to establish the dates and times for the summer Bible ministry. Find out when local community children's programs will be conducted. Then set a date and time that will not conflict dramatically with the local situation and will achieve the set goals.

Design a planning calendar

Develop a planning calendar that will direct your efforts for the coming weeks of preparation. Determine when you intend to do each step in preparation.

Preparation will be effective if you plan a calendar which reflects these guidelines:

- Five months in advance—set goals, select dates, time, curriculum, and design a planning calendar.
- Four months in advance—examine records from previous programs, design organization, begin recruitment.
- Three months in advance—complete recruitment, order curriculum (if needed).
- Two months in advance—train workers, begin publicity, arrange transportation.
- One month in advance—purchase supplies, conduct pre-registration, determine facilities, complete final details, finalize closing program (if planned), finalize follow-up plans.
- During the program—supervise, encourage, assist.
- After the program—carry out follow-up.

Create a workable organization

Plan the organizational structure for the program. If records are available, examine them from the last program to find the attendance patterns, curriculum used, personnel, and follow-up procedures. When calculating possible attendance figures, add to the previous figures to allow for new outreach. New students will likely follow a distribution similar to that of the previous program unless some special efforts are geared to a particular age group.

This information will help to determine how many classes (or sessions) to plan. On the whole, most summer programs require approximately:

1 leader per 4 to 5 preschoolers
1 leader per 6 to 8 elementary school children
1 leader per twelve teens

If yours is a large program, plan to recruit some department leaders to assist in recruiting, planning, and supervision.

List the other staff members needed to implement the program. The number and type of workers will vary according to the format and size of your summer Bible ministry program. These staff members might include assistants, craft leaders, recreational leaders, musicians, secretaries, transportation drivers, refreshment planners, devotional leaders, and purchasing agents.

Recruit and train staff

Begin early to recruit the staff. Make a list of all potential staff members. Find out who taught in previous programs. Make a list of those who teach Sunday school, youth groups, and midweek classes. Look over new member lists. Think of college students who will be home for the summer. Include high school students if you do not intend to conduct a program for teens. Consider available senior citizens. Then decide who will be the top choice for each position.

If you desire to build an excellent staff, ask them specifically, positively, and directly. Make a personal visit to those who are new recruits. Telephone calls may be all that is needed for those who are already involved in teaching in some area in the church educational program.

Although you will be assembling a worker pool for short term ministry, the need for training still exists. The varied experience levels among the staff, especially if many members are new to church education, will need some orientation. Training may be done (a) in several one to two hour sessions, (b) mornings or evenings once a month for 2 to 4 sessions, or (c) in a one-day session. How the training is done should be appropriate for the situation. But it must be done. (ETA's *Teaching with Confidence* age-level seminar materials could be used for training workers).

Publicize the program

Put adequate effort into publicity. A committee might carry out the publicity plans; but the program leader needs to meet with them to direct publicity toward meeting the stated goals.

Use every means appropriate to tell people about your summer Bible ministry program. The church newsletter, the Sunday bulletin, and the community newspaper are good ways to spread the word. Posters, both in the church building and in places of business, may be useful devices. Your imagination is the only limitation. Remember that personal contact with prospective students, however, is the most effective publicity device.

Plan for parental involvement

Family support and involvement in the program better insures attendance and continued support of future programs. How this is accomplished will vary according to the format and size of the summer Bible ministry program.

Most summer ministries provide news and announcements for the home through pamphlets, letters, and personal contact. Parents are encouraged to observe projects and help complete assignments given to their children.

Many summer programs that involve structured learning, albeit casual, also include a closing program. Again, if the program is large, a chairman may be selected to plan and direct it.

A good closing program is valuable. It need not be confined to a pageant-format in the church building. It may be a open house of learning areas used or perhaps a casual social setting. Some churches use this as an opportunity for an outdoor festival. Whatever style is used, participants have the opportunity to interact and share what they have learned. This should be a time when the value of outreach is demonstrated at its best.

The program may be developed around a unified theme with sub-groups (if applicable) contributing to a segment. Some closing programs feature a musical concert, drama, or multi-media presentation. Whatever the choice of program, it should be well planned. Every teacher and staff member should know their responsibilities.

Follow-up

Plan the follow-up procedures. Never assume that the results gained in your program will automatically continue without adequate follow-up.

Decide who will sort and store materials. Set a date for this to be completed. Perhaps all unused materials can be returned to the supplier for proper credit. Perhaps you prefer to donate items to the resource center of the church. Plan to return all equipment to its original location as well. You want to begin the fall programs with good will among all concerned.

Thank all the staff and other workers. This may be done with a public presentation, a coffee or luncheon. Or it may be done via telephone call, hand-written note, or more formal letter.

Complete all records. Store those that will be helpful to the next director or planning session. Make reports to the supervisory groups of the church.

Give the names of prospective teachers to appropriate leaders in other programs such as Sunday School, club programs, and youth groups.

Be sure that each participant is contacted after the session is over. Concentrate the major effort on new students who were contacted through the program(s). After the initial contacts have been made, give the names to evangelism committee members and the appropriate teachers in the congregation who can maintain communication throughout the year.

Summary

Summer Bible teaching ministries are as varied as the congregations that plan them. The church that takes summer programming seriously will find excellent outcomes if they plan carefully, publicize, and follow-up aggressively. Make summer an exciting teaching adventure in your church.

Review and discussion questions

1. What are the various types of summer Bible teaching ministries?
2. What are the advantages and disadvantages of each type summer Bible ministry?
3. What are the values of conducting summer Bible teaching ministries to the overall church educational program?
4. What are the steps in planning to conduct summer Bible teaching ministries?
5. How should a church determine the type of summer Bible ministry to conduct?
6. Why are summer Bible ministries effective in helping churches reach out into their communities?
7. Why is goal-setting basic to conducting a successful summer Bible teaching ministry?
8. Who should train new recruits to serve in summer Bible teaching ministries?

Application activities

1. Examine curriculum materials for summer Bible ministries from several suppliers. Decide which one would best carry out your goals for summer Bible teaching ministries.
2. Interview a previous director of a summer Bible ministry in your church. Decide what you should do the same and differently if you were asked to direct the next program.
3. Work out a planning calendar for the summer Bible teaching ministry in your church.

Vacation Bible school curriculum publishers

Concordia Publishing House
3558 S. Jefferson
St. Louis, MO 63118

David C. Cook Publishing
4050 Lee Vance View
Colorado Springs, CO 80918

Gospel Light Publications
2300 Knoll Ave.
Ventura, CA 93003

Gospel Publishing House
1445 Booneville Ave.
Springfield, MO 65802

National Baptist Publishing
7145 Centennial Blvd.
Nashville, TN 37209

Standard Publishing
8121 Hamilton Ave.
Cincinnati, OH 45231

Urban Ministries
1350 W. 103rd St.
Chicago, IL 60643

Vacation Venture Series
Christian Board of Publication
Box 179
St. Louis, MO 63166

General summer ministry materials

Betty Lukens Visuals
P.O. Box 2407
Rohnert Park, CA 94927-2407

CEF Press
P.O. Box 348
Warrenton, MO 63383-0348

Christian Family Video
1878 Firman Dr.
Richardson, TX 75081

Christian Video Enterprises
4101 NW 4th St., Suite 205
Plantation, FL 33317

Focus on the Family Publ.
8605 Explorer Dr.
Colorado Springs, CO 80920

Group Publishing
2890 N. Monroe
Loveland, CO 80538

Little Folk Visuals
39620 Entrepreneur Ln. #B
Palm Desert, CA 92211

CHURCH RETREATS AND CAMPING

6

Many churches are actively engaged in sponsoring church retreats and camping programs. These vital educational experiences are an important part of the church's Christian education ministry.

What are church retreats and camping programs?
Church retreats and camping programs are church-sponsored programs which include full-day learning experiences held in various settings and seek to fulfill appropriate Christian education objectives.

Benefits of retreats and camping programs

Church retreats and camping programs offer unique opportunities in Christian education. Their values are many and varied.

The different setting from other church activities, for instance, provides a fresh, natural environment in which people can prayerfully consider and reassess their Christian lives. Away from the pressures of peer groups, employment, and the hurried pace of present-day living, participants often make new decisions which impact their lives for years ahead.

Since retreats and camping programs usually provide for all-day experiences, these type programs offer an outstanding teaching potential for practical Christian living. As individuals relate to each other throughout the day in normal activities, Christianity becomes related to all of life.

Especially in children and youth programs, the leader-group relationship displays the witness of dedicated Christian counselors. This is undoubtedly one of the major influences of church-sponsored programs of this type. The normal daily routine of the camp or retreat provides many opportunities for counseling.

Those who have shared in Christian camp and retreat experiences consistently attest to their values. Both decisions to trust Christ and Christian growth result.

Types of retreats and camping programs

Even though both programs often have similar objectives, they also have unique characteristics that clearly distinguish each.

Retreats

Retreats are full-day Christian experiences. They are times for reflection, inspiration, and instruction that often involve an overnight stay. Although it is possible for retreats to be held almost anywhere, since most church facilities do not comfortably accommodate overnight stays, they are usually held in conference centers or at camp facilities.

Resident camp

The resident camp is conducted on a permanent site. Campers of various age levels (or families) live together for a specified period of time—usually one or two weeks. A long-term summer camp, however, may last as long as several months. Normally, permanent camp facilities are owned or used on a rental arrangement by the church group.

Trail or wilderness camp

The trail or wilderness camp has no permanent facilities, although it may be part of a resident camp program. Its basic characteristic emphasizes mobility, and sometimes is referred to as "trip camp." Modes of travel include backpack, bicycle, canoe, or horseback.

Day camp

Day camp, in which campers participate in programming on a daily basis with no overnight accommodations being provided, is a popular camping mode. This type of camp has many of the programmatic advantages of overnight camp, but is less expensive to operate. This kind of camping can be operated out of a church building taking advantage of local parks, pools, and other public facilities. It is ideal for ministering to young children and to children of families with both parents employed outside the home who must find summer programming for their children.

Specialty camps

A very popular form of either residential or day camping is the specialty camp. These camps combine Christian education and discipleship with training in a particular sport or skill. Examples of specialty camps include basketball, soccer, computer, study skills camp, weight reduction, and music.

Camps for special populations

Churches are increasingly becoming involved in ministry to persons with disabilities. Church buildings are being made handicapped accessible, special classes for the mentally handicapped are being formed, and church services interpreted for the hearing impaired. An often overlooked area of ministry to persons with disabilities is the camping ministry. Efforts can be made to mainstream campers with disabilities into a church's regular camp program or camps designed to meet the special needs of handicapped campers can be designed. Organizations such as Joni and Friends can help in planning an event which include persons with disabilities.

Relationship to other church ministries

Church retreats and camping programs are educational ministries of the church. As such, they usually are administered by the board of Christian education. Often retreat and camp arrangements will be a part of a broader denominational program or result from cooperation with other churches in the same geographical area.

It is important that all church ministries understand the potential of retreats and camping programs as supplementing and strengthening the total educational program. As in the case of summer Bible ministries, the seasonal aspects require that there be close relationships and follow-up through the other educational ministries to conserve results.

Organizing retreats and camping programs

Organizing a retreat or camping program is a challenging job involving many administrative details and cooperative teamwork. Developing the proper staff and program, securing appropriate facilities, follow-up, and financing all must be cared for in order to have an effective church retreat or camping program.

Those desiring more detailed information regarding organizing a retreat or camping program should consult some of the books listed in the bibliography or contact organizations such as Christian Camping International.

Personnel

Churches interested in an active retreat and camping program usually find it necessary to have a *camping and retreat coordinator* on the board of Christian education. This person's duties include such matters as planning camp and retreat programs, coordinating dates with the church schedule, guiding promotion, recruiting necessary personnel, and encouraging follow-through and follow-up. A *camping and retreat committee* can aid this person in performing these tasks. Qualifications for serving on the committee should include experience and well-developed organizational skills. If the proposed camping program is designed for or will include campers with disabilities, at least one member of the committee should have expertise in the area of disability of the campers. Special education teachers are often good candidates.

Program staff includes those with responsibilities in counseling and small group leading and all persons who deal directly with retreat participants or campers. A key task of the coordinator is recruiting, orienting, and training these people. Recruiting will be much easier if prospective program staff members know they will trained for their responsibilities. Too many people are recruited under the false pretense that "you really won't have to do much." If willing and capable staff cannot be found, the program should be postponed until all positions are filled.

A thorough training and orientation session several weeks before the event will pay off in staff confidence and effectiveness. Providing each staff member with a job description is also helpful. Developing job descriptions prevents misunderstanding and overlapping of responsibilities. These should include even the most obvious tasks.

Each staff member should be willing to make a time commitment. All staff members should be asked to give their time not only for the retreat or camp program, but for preplanning and follow-up as well. The time required for volunteer work should never be underestimated.

Program

Retreat and camping programming should provide a balanced schedule of educational, recreational, and fellowship activities. The program should not be something that happens just because it has happened before. Retreats and camp programs must have purposes and objectives. The coordinator and his/her committee should meet to develop a list of purposes and objectives prior to planning the program. Once the objectives are stated, the program flows from these statements.

All time should be scheduled from the point of departure for the retreat or camping facility until the participants return to their homes after the event. This includes activities on the bus or in the cars while traveling to and from the event, and all "free time." If persons with disabilities will be participating, extra time and personnel will need to be provided in the camp plan in order to accommodate their needs.

If an outside speaker is scheduled, inform him/her of the objectives for your program. The church retreat and camp program coordinator and his/her committee should suggest the topic or thrust of the speaker's messages. The objective for the retreat or camp should be the guiding factor in selecting a speaker. The temptation too often is to select a speaker who is popular—and then let him or her select the topics. If the program calls for certain objectives to be accomplished, however, the speaker must understand the importance of helping to meet those objectives.

While every coordinator or committee will want to prepare a personalized schedule, a sample for either a retreat or camping program might be:

8:00 Breakfast
9:00 Small-group Bible study
10:00 Morning instructional session
11:30 Recreational activity
12:30 Lunch
1:30 Afternoon instructional session
3:00 Recreational activities
5:00 Preparations for dinner
5:30 Dinner
7:00 Evening instructional session
8:30 Full-group fellowship and refreshments
9:30 In-room devotions

Of course, this schedule would vary for different age groups and program objectives, but fairly represents the basic elements of a daily program.

Facilities

Selecting a site is an important decision. Some groups enjoy using the same facility for each event while others like a variety of sites.

Select the site on the basis of the camp or retreat objectives. A facility with many tempting recreational areas and equipment will only frustrate retreat-goers or campers if the purpose of the program is to sit, listen, discuss, and think. On the other hand, if a large number of children or youth with much free time on the schedule has only one ping-pong table and a checkerboard, the group could get restless. Other factors to consider include weather, age of the participants, accommodations, travel time, facility regulations, and the possibility of sharing the site with other groups.

Any church using the facilities of an established residence camp or conference and retreat center needs to contact the director well in advance of the program and receive all the available information describing the facilities.

The church's retreat and camping coordinator and perhaps other members of his/her committee should also visit the facility in advance. Directors of these facilities prefer to meet with church retreat and camp coordinators and discuss the use of facilities. Careful planning will eliminate confusion and wasted time later. Touring the buildings noting room and campsite capacities will greatly help in planning. If persons with disabilities will be included, be sure that the facilities can accommodate them. Other items to be noted and discussed include menus, travel directions, parking areas, off-limits areas, camp rules, additional fees for activities, director's name, and emergency medical information.

If the facility has a contract, the church retreat and camp coordinator should obtain a copy in advance and read it to clarify any unclear details. Upon arrival, it is a good idea to tour the facility with a camp administrator and to note any damages existing before your group takes up occupancy. This can clear up any misunderstandings about responsibility for damages at the close of the camp.

Family and trip camping programs are becoming so popular, some churches have invested in such basic equipment as tents, lanterns, cooking utensils, and even sleeping bags. FIrst aid supplies top the list of essential items for any camping project.

Follow-up

To evaluate and follow-up the camp or retreat program, feedback from the participants and staff is essential. This can be done on a detailed prepared sheet or with an open-ended list of questions regarding good and bad points of the program. When responses are organized, the coordinator should prepare a report of the program to present to the board of Christian education and to file for future coordinators. Spiritual results should also be followed up by interviews and visits by support personnel or pastoral staff. All of this is just as important as the program itself.

Financing

Most camping and retreat facilities are financed through fees based on operating expenses. Fees are sometimes adjusted, however, on the basis of the participant's ability to pay. In order to provide a camp or retreat experience for everyone interested in attending, many churches provide "scholarships" which cover all, or part, of the fee for those otherwise unable to attend. Such scholarship funds may be in the church budget or they may be provided by church groups or personal gifts.

Camping and retreat planning committees should budget for a profit. In the case of a weekend retreat, for example, if the event costs $50, some groups charge $55 as an added precaution against unexpected expenses. A small surplus will also be available to use as a deposit for a future event.

Most camp and retreat facilities require a guarantee on the number of persons attending. If 100 persons are guaranteed, the church will be charged for 100. Retreat and camping coordinators might use some of these suggestions for avoiding unwarranted cancellations:
   - Requiring full payment in advance and no refunds for cancellations.
   - Requiring non-refundable deposits with a commitment to pay the full fee in the event of a last-minute cancellation.
   - Refunding of fees to emergency cancellations only if the camp or retreat facility allows some deviation from the final reservation count.

Summary

Church retreats and camping programs offer unique opportunities in Christian education. The setting, the full-day experience, and the close group relationship provide means for effective spiritual teaching and commitment to Christian life and living.

Major types of programs include weekend retreats, resident, day camps, specialty camps, and wilderness and trail camps.

Of vital importance in the success of the program are the church retreat and camping program coordinator, his/her committee, the staff, the purpose of the event, and the facilities.

Review and discussion questions

1. What are retreats and camping programs?
2. State two specific ways retreats and camping program can help your church.
3. Into what categories can retreats and camping programs be divided and what are the practical significance of these categories?
4. What are the distinctive values of these activities as educational ministries?
5. What reasons can be given for program committee and staff to be oriented and trained for their jobs?
6. What should be included in a daily retreat or camp schedule?
7. Why should the church retreat and camping program coordinator visit the facility prior to the event?
8. What organization is needed to carry on a retreat or camping program?
9. How can persons with disabilities be included in your camping program?

Application activities

1. Make a survey of a Bible book such as Genesis or Matthew and list those persons and events that might be interpreted as being related to a retreat or camping program.
2. Plan a rainy day program at a residence camp with a group of junior high campers.
3. Visit a retreat or camp facility and study its organization and operation procedures.

Organizations which help

Christian Camping Intl.
P.O. Box 62189
Colorado Springs, CO
80962-2189

Joni and Friends
P.O. Box 3333
Agoura Hills, CA 91301

ADULT
EDUCATION

7

The adult life span offers the church a major challenge for ministry. Persons 20 years of age and over, in most countries, comprise more than two-thirds of the total population. Recent statistics show that the average life span in these countries is 82 years for women and slightly less for men. If adulthood begins at approximately 20 years of age, simple arithmetic reveals that the church has to direct its educational planning to the changing patterns and needs of more than 60 years of adult life.

What is adult church education?
Adult church education is formal or informal activity which gives adults opportunities to learn, grow, or develop in their Christian lives.

Because the adult life span comprises a long period of time, it is necessary for churches to consider the characteristics of each adult and plan educational programs accordingly. In order to do this efficiently churches usually provide for adults in three major groups in the adult life span: older adult (approximately 60 years of age and up), middle adults (approximately 40-60 years of age), and young adults (approximately 20-40 years of age).

The gradual revolution of *older adult* involvement in our society demonstrates the interest of seniors in continuing a meaningful and productive life. As attitudes toward seniors change and more stereotypes of aging disappear, seniors seem to discover renewed freedom to remain involved.

Churches aware of the needs and potential of the older adult recognize that the issue facing the church is not how to care for the older adult (although it will have to do some of this); but, rather, how to restore a sense of purpose to the lives of seniors— many of whom have been set aside by the church.

For the *middle adult* the years between 40 and 60 are both a dreaded time and a time of potential. Many are aware that life is changing; but it is not clear why. These should be years of consolidation, evaluation, and inner renewal. Few adults, however, take the time to reflect on the changes taking place in their lives. Churches should recognize that adults in their 40s and 50s need to understand and relate to the transitions of this period.

Middle adults begin to feel the passage of time. Life is now structured in terms of life left to live. They question the meaning of life and are concerned that their lives may not have taken the right direction. Along with emotional evaluation, middle adults experience physical changes. The changes are similar to those of adolescence except they are in the reverse direction.

The *young adults* today are literally a new generation. Familiar program designations of "college and career," "young marrieds," and "singles" are less adequate in the contemporary church as program descriptions for young adults. College and career is no longer the exclusive domain of those 18-24 years of age and single and married young adults mix more readily than program separations will allow. Emerging trends in this age group need to be observed; but, it appears that young adults resist categories such as single, young marrieds, and college and career, when these programs isolate groups from one another.

Benefits of adult church education

Effective adult education in the local church accomplishes several benefits.

Encourages continuing growth

Effective adult education encourages the continuing growth of the adult through all of life. This fosters a sense of maturity throughout the church. Adults active in their own growth, learning, and ministry are more likely to be part of healthy relationships. They are also more likely to function capably and effectively in areas that require decision making.

Provides mature Christian adult role models

Adult education programs ensure the growth of adults who are able to act as models and mentors for the young. Children and youth in the church need the influence of adults who are modeling their faith in effective and public ways.

Fosters community outreach

Churches that have effective adult education programs foster outreach into the community. Growing adults are more aware of the need and more capable of effectively reaching out to others.

Develops continual leadership

Adult education continues the development of leadership. A balanced adult education program produces adults who are growing personally, growing in the knowledge of the Word, and growing in ministry and leadership skills. This can only serve to strengthen the church.

Types of adult education programs

Two factors need to be considered in planning and providing various types of adult education programs.

The first is to remember that adults usually prefer one particular way of learning (though they will participate in others). This method of learning is called andragogy and provides meaningful interaction with curriculum content on a personal level.

The second is that adults participate in educational programs for different reasons. Some adults learn for learning's sake. They will participate just the sake of hearing a lecture or joining a seminar. Other adults will not feel satisfied until the learning experience leads them to apply truth to real life situations. These adults (and this type of adult is in the majority) will not remain in learning experiences that are highly theoretical or that deal with content only. The third type of adult cares more about the personal relationships in the learning group. These adults will be attracted to groups that are building relationships between the participants.

Given the breadth of the adult life span, the variety of adult learning preferences, and the need to help adults deepen their biblical understanding and practice of the Christian faith—one adult Bible class on Sunday morning is not sufficient.

Sunday learning opportunities

Learning approaches can be varied on Sunday morning by using one or more of the following options:

Purposeful electives Create a sequence of courses and/or experiences that will help the church achieve its goals in adult education. Read the values of adult church education again. What courses or experiences could be provided to help accomplish these values? Following suggestions listed under guidelines for program content mentioned later in this chapter will also help in planning purposeful electives. Some churches plan a 3-4 year sequence of courses. This practice builds on the idea that adults will respond more positively to a program if they understand where it is taking them.

Short-term courses Six to eight week formats are proving more effective for adult education. It is easier to enlist a leader for a short term. And adults appreciate the "chewable bite." Outline course content in a six to eight week package—even though the course might deal with the same theme for 13 weeks.

Audio and videotape courses Resource centers and some theological schools offer audio and videotapes for use by local churches. Consulting a local Christian bookstore might help in locating these resources. Audio and video courses are especially helpful tools for group and individual instruction in churches whose adults enjoy learning from specialists.

Intergenerational courses Allowing persons of different ages and life situations to relate together in Bible learning or life-related learning has definite advantages. Create a short-term class (4-8 weeks) with a limited enrollment (12-16 persons). Invite youth and adults; young adults and older adults; middle adults and high schoolers; young couples and senior adults; or any other combination. Local Christian bookstores can help in locating some resources available in planning intergenerational courses.

Specialized courses promoted according to the teaching method For example, schedule two courses dealing with the Gospel of Mark. Point out that one course will be taught by lecture with a minimum of discussion and that the other will utilize an inductive approach including real-life practice of issues from the gospel. To accomplish these objectives, be sure to invite instructors who are particularly skilled in the method used in the course.

Mini-terms Utilize a period in the church year that lends itself to mini-term courses. For example. many churches would profit from a four-week study unit during Advent or an expanded Easter study that fills an entire month preceding Resurrection Sunday. Since January is often a difficult month for teachers and learners, other churches might use the intersession approach then or a video series which involves the entire adult population in the church. Having a series of lessons which runs during "J" months is another idea. Every month beginning with a "J" is an opportunity for a mini-course taught to a larger or specialized group of adults (e.g. single parents).

Supplementary learning experiences

Enhance adult education programming by including one or more of the following options.

Independent learning opportunities for individual adults Design a brochure featuring several books that any adult who wants to can study independently. Toward the end of the unit, schedule a round-table discussion in which all adults reading a particular book can come together and discuss their insights. Or make quality tapes available to adults who can use them as they drive or listen to them at home. Arrange for these adults of come together at an appointed time to discuss the content of the tape.

Morning or afternoon programs for seniors Many seniors are not comfortable leaving their homes in the evening. Create experiences that will allow for a variety of opportunities for seniors during the day—Bible studies, craft classes, seminars, travelogues, hot lunches.

Sunday noon "tabletalks" Adults will often stay for lunch rather than come out on a weekday evening. Use these settings for fellowship; calling out a particular group for ministry (e.g. those who would be caregivers); or addressing a particular group (e.g. developing the potential of the senior years or building the single parent support groups).

Noon hour seminars Create these experiences for adults in a similar workplace location or at a university or college campus.

All-day clinics The clinic deals with a specific skill rather than trying to cover an entire area in one day (e.g. storytelling or how to study the Bible).

Training vacation Invite adults to give 1-2 weeks of their vacation at a camp setting. Create a family camp including opportunities for single adults, single parents, seniors. The family camp setting will help accommodate the needs of the children. Use the time for fellowship, planning, skill development, inspiration, problem solving.

Relationship to other church ministries

It is important for leaders in planning adult education programs to relate to other ministries. For example: those who plan for children, youth, and adults need to discuss the potential of family ministry. Adult leaders need to become aware of the education programs being provided in other areas in order to develop realistic program development options for adults. If seminars in worship, prayer, or missions are planned, they will have to be developed with others who use the building and provide services in these content areas. Also, the librarian or media center director will need to know the adult education resources needed.

Organizing adult education

As with other areas of church education, it is important to consider the personnel, program, facilities, and financing of the adult educational program.

Personnel

Adult education leaders are not as ready to become involved in ministry and programs that require long-term commitment. Many of their reasons are legitimate. Creative ways of allowing adult education leaders to become involved in situations that suit their time, gifts, and interest must be found. For example: invite adults to become part of a teaching team that works together to teach a course (one adult may be more suited to presenting content in interesting ways; another may be more skillful in leading a group discussion, decision making, or problem solving; another in building personal relationships; another in bringing creative dimension to the teaching experience).

Listen to those who are capable of teaching adults. How do they want to serve? Begin with the assumption that they want to serve the Lord and more leaders will respond positively.

Program

As mentioned earlier in this chapter, consider planning a balanced program of adult education using a broad variety of learning formats. Ask "What input does an adult require in order to continue growth to maturity?" The following general categories of input might prove helpful in planning content for adult education.

Learning the Bible and theology Include courses that provide overviews of important areas of Scripture. Provide experiences for the new believer, the unbeliever, the more mature Christian. Courses in ethics, church history, apologetics, and doctrine are also needed. Help adults deepen their understanding of the Bible and biblical subjects.

Growing in Christian life disciplines Provide experiences that will help adults develop skills in prayer, Bible study, and witnessing.

Equipping for ministry It is possible for most adults to go through their entire church experience without receiving significant training in a ministry area; or without ever being approached on a one-to-one basis concerning their ministry potential. Be deliberate in planning courses and experiences that will further ministry development for all adults.

Working through life cycle concerns Where better to deal with issues such as family life, singleness, single parenting, aging, mid-life crisis, divorce, death and dying than in the church? Adults will experience a great variety of life cycle concerns through their lives. Be sensitive to these and provide the forum that will allow adults to talk together about their needs and challenges.

Learning to live a part of the Christian community Adults need to learn what it means to be part of the church and the larger Christian community. Include effective missions experiences, seminars on worship, on what it means to pray together as the Christian community, or on how to solve problems.

Facilities

Obviously, the church sanctuary is not the most suitable place for all that has to happen in learning with adults. Small churches may need to consider using other locations (e.g. a room in a restaurant or a local hotel, space in a school, or a family room in someone's home). It may be possible to add a portable building on the church site. Some churches have even removed the fixed pews from their sanctuaries and substituted comfortable, moveable chairs to allow more flexibility in the use of that large space.

When planning a new building, consider the design of spaces that will allow for a variety of uses. Create a room for the more formal approaches (lecture, seminars, etc.) Include tables, a projection screen, a public address system if necessary, good lighting, and comfortable chairs. Also design a room that can be

used for more informal groupings. Build a fireplace; add uphol-
stered furniture; and heavy-duty wiring for the coffee maker,
teakettle or small hotplate, and compact refrigerator. Also plan
for rooms that can be used for small group work or counseling.

Financing

List all the areas included under the general topic of adult
education. What resources are needed? Are special speakers
necessary? Will the church have to rent space or purchase equipment? Should the church pay the fees for some adult leaders to
attend seminars? Specify each area requiring financial assistance.
Then develop a list of finances needed for adult education and
submit it to the church budget committee. Remember, when
specific needs are listed, finances are more likely to be provided.

Summary

The nature of the adult life span dictates a need for variety in
planning. General learning and ministry can take place across the
life span, while age-related needs can be met in specific seminars.
Because of the breadth of the adult life span and diverse learning
preferences, a variety of learning options is necessary and
possible.

Review and discussion questions

1. Why is it important for churches to plan for adult education?
2. What types of adult educational programs are needed in the
   church?
3. What are some differences in planning for the major age
   groupings of adults?
4. How does the adult education program relate to other parts
   of the church program?
5. What are suggested guidelines for developing adult education
   in the church?
6. How much variety in format and content would be appropriate and appreciated in your church?
7. How can an awareness of the need of adults to continue their
   growth and learning be promoted in your church?
8. List ways to get feedback from adults concerning your
   church's adult education program.

Application activities

1. Analyze your congregation. What is the average age of your
   membership? What proportion of your congregation are older
   adults? Middle adults? Young adults? How many young families do you have in your church? Families with teenagers?
   Families where middle-aged children and aging parents live
   together? How would you characterize the level of Bible
   knowledge in your church? Mature Christian? New Christian?

2. Speak to a sampling of adults of different ages and Christian experience. What needs and opportunities for adult education can you discern? What insights for developing an adult education program can they offer?
3. Assess the learning opportunities available to adults in your church. What are their strengths? What can you do to improve them?

YOUTH PROGRAM

8

The youth program is one of the church's key educational challenges for it provides Christian guidance for young people during some of their most crucial decision-making years. Reaching and holding young people with an effective youth ministry requires thorough planning and dedicated effort.

Youth program planners need to remember that teenagers want action and many feel the church ministry for young people is inadequate in this area. The action, however, must be part of a balanced program and carefully related to the church's Christian education objectives.

Today's teenagers face more complex problems than ever before. The church is challenged to guide this generation for the cause of Christ and an effective youth program provides one practical means to this end.

What are church youth programs?
Church youth programs are church-sponsored, organized activities, specifically designed for young people, which provide leadership development, Christian fellowship, and service opportunities.

Benefits of youth programs

Youth programs have at least five outstanding benefits:
- They provide opportunity for training as teens assume leadership roles while being guided in them.
- They encourage wholesome, satisfying social experiences, an important part of a young person's life.
- By group and personal guidance in spiritual growth and concerns, young people are helped to move from spectator to participant roles in dealing with their concerns.
- Youth programs also open doors to meaningful Christian service, with implications for future faithfulness.

57

- Witnessing for Christ is one of the basic objectives of an effective youth program as teens learn to share their faith.

Types of youth programs

Although the aim of bringing young people together for involvement and leadership opportunities not available in other areas of church education remains the same, youth programming recently has taken on much greater diversity. Most youth programs can be divided into three categories.

Sunday evening programs

The Sunday evening program usually precedes or follows an evening service. Maximum involvement is the key with young people sharing in planning, directing, and presenting group meetings or fellowship opportunities.

Weekday programs

Some churches conduct activities at other times during the week. Informal recreation, social events, or service opportunities in the evening can be followed by a fellowship, devotional, or Bible study program.

Combination

To provide the maximum amount of opportunity for both spiritual growth and leadership training, some churches have combined the traditional Sunday evening program with activities on another evening. Many of these churches dedicate the Sunday evening program to spiritual and leadership development and the midweek program to outreach, fun activities, and fellowship.

Churches whose physical plants include a gymnasium find this combination approach to be especially effective.

Relationship to other church ministries

If the youth program is to be effective and productive, it must distinctively contribute to church education and work cooperatively with the other educational ministries to provide balanced coverage of biblical truth, Christian living, and service experiences. While the church service is basically for worship and Sunday school for instruction, the youth program features involvement through ministry and training. All three blend together into a coordinated learning experience.

The youth program is not a substitute for the home, but must cooperate with the home in equipping today's teens for their future roles as mature Christian adults, parents, and leaders.

Organizing youth programs

Church youth program organizers should include as many of the following formula elements as possible in their plans.

Concerned and trained adult leaders
+ a group of participating young people
+ a functional organizational pattern
+ a stimulating program curriculum
+ careful, long-range plans
+ much cooperative work

= a successful youth leadership program

Personnel
Dedication to the Lord demonstrated by a vibrant Christian experience and a sincere passion for young people are important qualifications for adult youth leaders. Also important are the ability to adapt to changing situations, a sense of humor, patience, a willingness to sacrifice time and skills in organizing and following through on plans and program.

As with other educational ministries, before searching for possible youth leaders be sure the program's objectives are in order and job descriptions have been developed. All persons being recruited should also have identified and demonstrated the appropriate spiritual gift(s) to be successful in ministering to youth and have felt God's call to youth ministry.

Many churches also provide an equipping/training seminar for youth leaders. ETA has an effective seminar program to accomplish this need titled *Teaching Youth with Confidence.*

In their attempts to recruit qualified youth workers, many churches find that a married couple or a man and a woman serving as team leaders has advantages over just one leader. This provides an adviser for the particular concerns of both sexes. It also allows a broader sharing of responsibilities.

Teen leaders elected by a group usually include a president, secretary, treasurer, and social chairperson. Depending upon the size of the group, additional leaders might include vice president and chairpersons in charge of any other program elements such as: missions, visitation, or promotion.

Program
Programs for church youth groups have many elements that contribute to their effectiveness.

Leadership opportunities Leadership is developed by actively involving people in leading, so the youth program is really a laboratory situation. Adult advisers may produce more polished and better organized meetings and activities, but it is more important to enable the youth to develop their own leadership skills.

Program variety Youth programs should meet the needs of contemporary teens. Such vital topics as dating, courtship, marriage, honesty, temptation, vocational choice, choice of music, race relations, witnessing, and Christian doctrines may be considered. Meaningful and honest answers emerge from the young people themselves through a variety of methods, including debates, panel discussions, quizzes, simulations, drama, interviews, and demonstrations.

Planning groups In order to develop leadership qualities, the young people can be divided into groups to plan and organize youth activities. These planning groups vary according to the size of the youth ministry. The goal is to get as many young people to participate as possible. To accomplish this goal at least two groups are essential for most youth programs.

Planning groups provide greater involvement for more young people. The teens should be divided into groups providing for a balance of abilities, experience, and leadership with an adult adviser assigned to each group.

Specialized programming Many churches find that special programs tied to teen interests provide opportunities for youth to develop their abilities and to reach out. The focus can be either evangelism or discipleship. Musical groups, drama teams, and interest groups are just a few of the possibilities.

Youth leaders must be aware of the varied interest and intensity of involvement youth are seeking. Some teens want to be heavily involved and discipled while others wish only to attend regularly, occasionally, or not at all.

Social experiences Learning to live and work cooperatively is a skill all need to acquire. Social activities can offer learning opportunities and means of Christian witness. While fellowship itself is a legitimate objective, alert and informed adult leaders can often guide the group into other objectives as well. A post-athletic game fellowship, for example, can be a practical means of reaching non-Christian students. A social such as a fun night created without announcement can give guidance for using leisure time.

Some general suggestions for planning social activities are:
- Determine the social needs of the group members.
- Organize the needs into major categories, relating to specific social activities.
- List the potential social activities available to the youth.
- Program one major and one minor social event each month.
- Plan the events with the youth.
- Evaluate each event immediately after it has taken place.
- Repeat tested activities and try new ones.

Guidance A great need in working with young people is for teens and adult leaders to communicate. Today's youth are searching for this kind of honest guidance to stay balanced in an ever-changing world. To accomplish the level of communication needed, effective adult leaders should establish a relationship of trust with the young people. The adult leader who desires to counsel teens meaningfully listens to them, sees problems from their point of view, and helps teens find answers by supporting, clarifying, or just offering an available ear. Effective Christian counselors are not too quick to advise, yet not reticent to explain what the Bible says about their counselees' concerns.

Guidance can be planned and/or unplanned. Informal counseling happens in the car as you drive along on outings and at athletic events when casual remarks are exchanged and attitudes displayed. Through casual conversations, vital issues are raised in a permissive environment. Informal contact can be the most influential factors in counseling youth.

More formal guidance sessions can also be considered. One way to do this is to announce a regular program of individual counseling. A carefully selected place and regular appointments are needed. The counselor should have available a variety of print materials on major youth concerns to distribute as needed. A simple, orderly interview agenda can be used to give direction to the session. Friendliness, concern, and sincere interest in the young person should radiate through the session.

This counseling involves such areas as spiritual help, vocational guidance, or other concerns that can be handled by a mature Christian adult. More serious matters should be referred to the pastor or a professional counselor.

Service opportunities Helping young people put their learning into practice is also important. The church has many service opportunities. A few of the ways young people can minister are: serving as helpers and leaders in summer Bible ministries, helping with church office duties, caring for buildings and grounds, visiting people who are confined at home or in institutions, serving meals or participating in services at a rescue mission, witnessing or distributing tracts at street meetings, participating in worship services and children's programs.

"Use me or lose me" has been the call of youth; but too few churches have responded. Teens can and want to meaningfully contribute to the life of the local church.

Facilities and materials

Ideal facilities for youth activities include rooms for sports and socials, perhaps a gymnasium, as well as a comfortable place for regular meetings. Unfortunately few churches have all these, but with creativity, investigation, and work, suitable facilities are possible.

Materials are another key to a productive program. Both adult leaders and youth need to have available resource materials on the relevant issues confronting today's Christian teens. Involvement and growth come from motivational youth programs that help teens find Christian answers to today's perplexing problems.

When selecting program materials, keep the following guidelines in mind:
- Are the subjects meaningful to youth?
- Do the materials allow youth to develop biblical answers?
- Are the materials easy enough for a teen to present yet aimed at helping them cultivate leadership skills and spiritual discernment?
- Does the curriculum present a wide range to topics in an orderly manner?
- Do the materials correlate with those used in other church ministries?

Financing

Young people can often finance their youth program from funds given in offerings and through special youth fund-raising projects. In churches where fund-raising is not permitted and an expanded program is desired, churches budget for youth programming and provide such help as camp scholarships.

Summary

The church faces an increasing challenge to develop Christian leadership abilities in its youth. Traditional church youth programs can still be used effectively for this.

The concept of a laboratory situation is especially pertinent. Youth learn best when programming materials and methods involve the group members and when program topics are practical and deal with teen interests and needs. Biblical truths will become meaningful as they are applied to everyday experiences.

Adult leaders provide mature guidance for teens and encourage their Christian initiative and leadership growth. Opportunities for service and purposeful social experiences also cultivate this growth.

Review and discussion questions

1. Why should churches have programs for youth other than Sunday school?
2. Identify today's teens' greatest needs.
3. What elements contribute to a successful leadership program for young people?
4. What characteristics should an adult leader have to effectively help today's teens meet their needs?
5. What type social program should a church provide for youth?
6. How can the church's youth program help parents and teens to communicate more effectively?
7. How can a local church develop an effective guidance program for its youth?
8. In what ways can young people serve the Lord in and through the local church?

Application activities

1. Visit a Sunday evening youth program in another local church. Study it from the standpoint of adult leadership, youth involvement, and program adequacy.
2. Interview five teens concerning their interest in the church's total program specifically centering on their recommendations for the youth program.
3. How is your church helping youth coming from broken homes and different family situations to cope?
4. Chart the relationships between the various parts of your church's total youth program. Use solid lines to show what relationships presently exist and broken lines to illustrate what relationships should be added.

Organizations which help

Church leaders needing help in setting up or finding curriculum resources for use in their youth programs might contact: their Sunday school curriculum publisher, one of the organizations listed at the end of the chapter on boys and girls club programs, their denominational educational offices or publishing houses, or any of the interdenominational organizations that provide youth curriculum materials and/or leadership training resources.

Group Books
2890 N. Monroe
Loveland, CO 80538

Positive Action for Christ
P.O. Box 1948
Rocky Mount, NC 27802-1948

Serendipity House
8100 Southpark Way Unit A-6
Littleton, CO 80120

Sonlife Ministries
1119 Wheaton Oaks Court
Wheaton, IL 60187

Youth for Christ/USA
P.O. Box 228822
Denver, CO 80222

Youth Specialities
Zondervan Publishing House
5300 Patterson Ave. SE
Grand Rapids, MI 49530

BOYS AND GIRLS CLUB PROGRAMS

9

Clubs are fun—ask any boy or girl. They bring children into the church program and open challenging doors for Christian witnessing, teaching, and training.

Christ-centered weekday programs afford the local church an opportunity to enhance the foundation of biblical knowledge acquired in the Sunday school. Secular influence, with relative moral standards and disintegrating home life, bombards impressionable young lives every day. Many children who are not related to any other church educational ministry can be reached through club programs. Their participation in the local church grows from there. Children who are a part of the local body gain valuable guidance in expressing their faith with friends.

What are children's clubs?
Church clubs for boys and girls are church-sponsored, organized programs of wholesome recreation and achievement whose biblical emphasis leads to new life and growth in Christ.

Benefits of weekday activity programs

Club programs for children have many benefits for the local church. Among them are community outreach, Christian character building, Bible teaching, spiritual growth, and meeting the needs of the whole person.

Community outreach

"May I go to the club program at church tonight?" asks a ten-year-old from an unchurched home. When he arrives, the boy finds activities which match his desire for action and fun and genuine interest and friendship on the part of the club leaders. But he also learns the message of the gospel. Effective club programs are designed to eventually lead this boy into new life in Christ.

Here is a child, with no previous relationship to church or Sunday school, being reached through a club format. Not only is he reached but a contact has been made that could extend to the entire family.

Christian character building

A club program is a ministry which helps Christian children grow in the Lord. Through group activities club members learn to practice Christian principles of behavior and leadership. And through play, children's characters are molded and their moral qualities are developed.

The need for fun and recreation is met in a Christian atmosphere, and new skills and creative abilities are developed in working with practical crafts and hobbies.

Teaching the Bible

Club programs fit into church education because they teach the Word of God. Materials must be Bible-based and doctrinally sound. In a club program, Scripture memory should be taught on the child's level of understanding and its application kept practical. Many times a meaningful discussion of a memory verse leads to a spiritual counseling session. An effective program will also strengthen habits of personal Bible study and encourage club members to establish private daily devotions.

Spiritual growth through example and counsel

Leaders have much contact with children in club activities. Their Christian character and example must show through in normal, informal ways. As the club members become acquainted with their leaders, friendship and fellowship are strengthened; and opportunity for spiritual counseling increases. Children who have confidence in the sincerity and spirituality of their leaders will more freely share their own problems and accept counsel.

At the same time, the leaders see the children and youth in a natural situation. Problems come to the surface and needs are more clearly manifested.

Reaching the whole person

The church's program should be developed in terms of its ministry to whole persons. If church education programs are to be effective, they must be balanced with a proper emphasis on instruction, worship, witness, testimony, fellowship, and service. Programs that minister to physical, social, and emotional needs, in additional to the mental and spiritual, demonstrate the church's interest in the total person. A Christ-centered program will be concerned with developing well-integrated, Christian personalities. A carefully planned club program leads to an appreciation of all aspects of life being related to God. This will result in integration of life around the center—Christ.

Types of activity programs

Churches becoming involved in club programs usually join with one of the national organizations or develop their own programs.

National organizations

Many churches prefer to adopt a club program that is already clearly outlined, developed, and proven successful. Such programs are available from organizations whose purpose is to serve the local church. Examples of interdenominational organizations include Adventure Clubs and Awana Youth Association (all ages), Christian Service Brigade (boys only), Pioneer Clubs (for boys and girls), and Exciting Bible Clubs (known as Space Cubs, Whirlybirds, and Jet Cadets). Some churches have worked with the scouting program, adding their own spiritual emphasis and Bible content. Some denominations incorporate theologically distinctive studies to develop their own programs.

Established clubs have the advantage of experience-tested, well-balanced formats and necessary support materials. Also available are helpful services from the sponsoring organization. Affiliation with a large national organization may also prove attractive to recruiting new church members who would be familiar with the program at another location.

Individual church programs

If a church prefers to develop its own program, this may be done by focusing on a special emphasis. Sports, music, drama, hobbies, handcraft projects, or whatever combination of activities would meet local needs could also be a point of development. Sometimes an existing educational program, such as the Sunday school or youth group, is expanded to include regular midweek activities.

Some churches, particularly those without the denominational support of a training hour, will find a need to provide opportunities for experience in Christian lifestyle skills. Local church-designed club programs seek to organize an eclectic list of needs. Structured sessions are built around themes and emphasize participation in many of the same practical skills found with the national organizations.

Commonly built upon any block of time when other family members are gathering for other purposes, these clubs schedule a variety of activities for children. Since the building is already reserved for use, it may be considered stewardship wise to include children's activities.

To assume the task of developing your program, a capable church staff is usually necessary to gather and analyze support materials from various independent publishing houses, such as Rainbow Publishers or Shining Star Publications, that specialize in elective study materials. The major curriculum publishers, and some denominational publishers, also carry an array of elective products to enhance the overall program for children. Music materials, such as Maranatha *Kids' Praise*, Lillenas *Sing a Song of Scripture*, WordKids, and Brentwood Kids Company all produce topical issues in a musical format.

Whichever pattern is chosen, careful planning, proper leadership, and adequate supervision are essential.

Relationship to other church ministries

A club program should not duplicate or overlap the work of other educational ministries, but rather supplement them. Its unique emphasis, in terms of program elements, is not found in formal instruction and worship; but in fellowship and purposeful learning activity. It is not another Sunday school or worship service; but a social, recreational, and participatory program designed to appeal to children's interests and needs.

The club program should be organized and administered as a part of the total church educational program for children. As such, it follows the same supervision of church staff or board of Christian education. Usually club directors serve on the Christian education board or other advisory role. Churches that are organized by age-group divisions (children, youth, adults) administer the club program within the appropriate divisional organization.

Organizing club programs

As with other educational ministries, the personnel, program, facilities, equipment, and financing are important in the organization of club programs.

Personnel

The effectiveness of a club program depends upon its leadership. Recruiting competent leaders is a matter of prayer, promotion, and persistence. When leaders are enthusiastic and programs are well publicized, club programs meet their objectives and grow.

Leaders who are effective with children are young at heart. They know and identify with the age group they work with and generally enjoy life and living. In the words of Paul, they "must not be quarrelsome, but be kind to all, able to teach, patient..." (2 Tim. 2:24).

Christian leadership requires spiritual maturity. Often individuals with a special interest in club activities, even though they are young in the faith, can be used as assistant leaders as they "grow in grace." Key leaders, however, should be mature Christians with a deep sense of spiritual responsibility.

Club leaders need training in order to serve effectively. Club leadership usually requires special knowledge of meetings, activities, games, achievement work, and other aspects of the program. Most national club organizations require some training and testing of potential leaders and are happy to assist the church in this vital task.

Program

Successful programs include activities which are geared to the age level. This implies graded programs for children.

When the church is using a denominational or interdenominational plan, the program is already established and materials available. Usually these programs are balanced in recreational activities, individual achievement work, and spiritual teaching. Some flexibility exists for the local church who may wish to augment a portion more or less than is prescribed. Most club meetings are held weekly, with older club members meeting separate from younger groups. This is especially advisable as a safety precaution to the young. Other activities such as hiking and camping are often included in the program as well.

A key part of most established programs is developing youth leadership. This involves both personal achievement work and practical leadership opportunities in the meetings.

In club programs, boys and girls are most often grouped separately to promote more personal dialogue during the inspirational and life application portions. Activities which develop ideals and standards help both groups in future coeducational activity.

Facilities and equipment

Elaborate facilities are not necessary. However, a basic physical activity area for club meetings and storage space for game equipment, handcraft or hobby supplies is essential. Most churches have a basement area or multi-purpose room that can be adapted for club activities. Others may find school or community facilities available.

Financing

As a vital part of the total church ministry, club programs should be adequately addressed in the church educational budget. The participants usually buy their own materials and uniforms (if used) so the basic investment for the church normally includes only recreational equipment, initial supplies of materials, and rental of facilities when necessary.

Summary

Club programs help meet basic needs in the lives of active children and youth. When properly correlated with the total church educational program, they assist in accomplishing the basic objectives of Christian education—evangelism, edification, and equipping for Christian service.

Many churches are reaping rich dividends in terms of lives reached for Christ because they invested in a program that considers children's needs and interests and ministers to the total individual.

Review and discussion questions

1. Why program weekday activities?
2. Why should a church provide clubs for its children?
3. What types of club activity can be used in the church?
4. What is the relationship of a club program to the Sunday school?
5. What place will the Bible have in a club program?
6. How can clubs be fully correlated with other ministries of the church educational programs?
7. Discuss the potential for informal contact and personal counseling in a club program.
8. Discuss the advantages and disadvantages of adopting an established club program as compared to designing your own.
9. List and discuss the distinctive aspects of club programs, as compared to Sunday school classes.
10. What facilities, equipment, and finances are required for a club program?

Application activities

1. Visit and evaluate a club program in another church.
2. Write the headquarters of a national club organization for information concerning its programs.
3. Interview several leaders in a club program observing their handling of the activities.
4. Talk to several club members in your church. Ask them what they like best about their club, and what they would like to change in their club's program.

Organizations which can help

Accent Publications
P.O. Box 15337
Denver, CO 80215-0337

Adventure Clubs
D. C. Cook Publishing Co.
4050 Lee Vance View
Colorado Springs, CO 80918

Awana Youth Association
1 East Bode Road
Streamwood, IL 60107

BCM International
237 Fairfield Ave.
Upper Darby, PA 19082-2299

Brentwood Kids Company
One Maryland Farms Ste. 200
Brentwood, TN 37027

Christian Service Brigade
765 Kimberly Drive
Carol Stream, IL 60188

Exciting Bible Clubs
C.E. / Rainbow Publishers
PO Box 261129
San Diego, CA 92196-1129

Good News Clubs
Child Evangelism Press
P.O. Box 348
Warrenton, MO 63383

Integrity Music Just For Kids
1000 Cody Rd.
Mobile, AL 36695

Kids' Praise
Maranatha Music/Benson Dist.
30230 Rancho Viejo Rd.
San Juan Capistrano, CA 92675

Lillenas Publishing Co.
P.O. Box 419527
Kansas City, MO 64141

Pioneer Clubs, Inc.
P.O. Box 788
Wheaton, IL 60189-0788

Shining Star Publications
1204 Buchanan Street
PO Box 399
Carthage, IL 62321-0399

Success With Youth
(see Exciting Bible Clubs)

Word of Life Fellowship, Inc.
P.O. Box 600
Schroon Lake, NY 12870-0600

CHILDREN'S CHURCH

10

Children's church offers opportunity for children to participate in worship on their level. It is the primary component in the church's educational ministry for instructing children in worship.

A definition of worship provides the reason a church should develop an effective children's church. The believer should view worship as a one-on-one communion with God. When believers comprehend what God has done for them in the supreme sacrifice of Jesus Christ, for the redemption of their souls they are compelled to respond to God in His utmost love, respect, honor, and submission. When God redeemed mankind, He did so for the ultimate purpose of communion with Him. Thus, it is important that children's church be designed to instruct children regarding who God is, who and why people worship Him, and how God expects His children to worship Him.

Educationally sound and spiritually profitable, children's church not only teaches children Bible content; but also provides a practical foundation for future church relationships. Children's church is not another Sunday school nor does it seek to provide merely a child care program.

What is children's church?
Children's church is a Sunday morning worship activity for children, whereby they have the opportunity to worship God on the level of their understanding. Children's worship is ideally held simultaneously with the adult worship or during a portion of that time and should be modeled after it.

At one time children's church programs for any age group were called "junior church." As interest in the ministry increased, closer grading developed and divisions now often follow the same pattern as Sunday school: preschool church, primary church, and junior church.

71

Churches with sufficient children have found separate children's choirs to be an attractive feature of the children's church program. These choirs may periodically minister in song to the adult church congregation, thus sharing the children's church ministry with the entire church.

Other areas of children's church ministry might be putting on short musical dramas, choral readings, memorizing and reciting portions of the Scriptures. Instrumental music by proficient and well-prepared children, special music (solos, duets, ensembles, etc.) which are guided and prepared by a trained musician.

Benefits of children's church

Children's church has many benefits. It provides children with meaningful worship experiences, clarifies worship activities, strengthens adult church services, and develops family church worship.

Meaningful worship experiences

Children's churches are primarily designed to teach children how to worship and provide children with meaningful worship experiences. Recognizing the children's level of understanding, children's church helps them establish and reinforce their relationship to God through prayer, music, giving, serving, sharing, and Bible study.

Clarifies worship activities

Few activities in life become significant patterns of behavior without instruction and preparation. A child's conduct in church can become purely imitative and superficial. Children's church provides one solution. Here, in early formative years, young Christians are taught the attitudes as well as the actions of congregational worship.

Children's church is in keeping with the principles enunciated in Proverbs 22:6, "Train up a child in the way he should go, even when he is old he will not depart from it."

Strengthens adult church service

Too few adults really know how to worship. One reason is the lack of training in worship during their childhood years. Young people being developed in a properly functioning children's church program will be able to participate more intelligently in adult worship activities.

Develops family church worship

An outstanding advantage of children's church is how it contributes to family worship. While children's church can divide the family pew, it more frequently unites the family. Parents who previously took turns missing church rather than try to discipline uninterested small children can now attend church together.

Family discussion should be encouraged after church to demonstrate parent's interest, concern, and reinforcement. This also assures the child that parents and leaders/teachers are a team working together on their behalf.

Parents are ultimately responsible for their children's education and development and this provides an opportunity to build continuity, agreement, and confirmation of God's will for our lives (Deut. 6:8).

A well-programmed children's church provides for periodic church attendance by children with their parents, allowing entire families to attend church together when this may not normally be possible. As children attend portions of the regular service with their parents, a gradual oneness of family worship is developed. Parents can also follow-up what their children are learning in children's church during these times if the purpose and program of children's church is explained to them.

Types of children's churches

Although similar in purposes, children's churches vary in format, length, and age level.

During entire worship service

When multiple children's churches meet during the entire time of the adult worship service, a number of separate rooms are necessary. Full-length children's churches provide for maximum participation in planning and presenting the worship program.

Although preschool children's church is generally held during the adult worship time, the older children sometimes participate in the regular worship service one Sunday a month. On that Sunday a children's choir might sing and the pastor will keep his young hearers in mind as he preaches.

During part of the church service

In this plan, children are with their families or sitting together as a group during the worship service, up to the time of the sermon. Then, during a hymn or other musical interlude, they go to their own meeting place for the rest of the worship time.

A second variation is to have a brief children's message included in the regular service, often just before the children leave for their own worship activities. Careful planning of the children's church topics can provide for correlation with the sermon.

Varied according to age groups

Children's church may be divided in a number of ways. A common age division is:

Preschool church—ages 2-5 (preschool and kindergarten)
Primary church—ages 6-8 (grades 1-3)
Junior church—ages 9-11 (grades 4-6)

The extent of each group's participation in the adult worship service can be determined by its ability to participate meaningfully.

Relationship to other educational ministries

Children's church is part of the total church program. As such, the doctrines and policies of the church are the same for the children's church. Church pastors are children's church pastors, although the pastor's personal participation may be limited. To better reinforce this concept, occasionally the pastor might visit the children's church and pray with them to give his encouragement and support to this work.

Leaders of church activities for children should also be aware and supportive of other children's programs. Duplication of lessons and activities can be avoided if the board of Christian education is effectively correlating the curriculum of all the children's ministries in the church.

Organizing children's church

The organization of children's church includes the personnel, program, facilities and equipment, and financing.

Personnel

The children's church director is normally appointed by the board of Christian education. He/she works with the pastor, minister or director of Christian education, or children's director in selecting workers and general planning.

Planning should begin by carefully stating the objectives for the children's church program, formulating a job description for each position in the children's church ministry, earnestly praying for guidance, and carefully searching for those leaders who already feel called of God to minister to children. It is important that children's church leaders possess the skills and attributes needed in guiding children into true worship of God. The leaders should be just as dedicated, consistent, and godly in their Christian walk as any other church leader and exhibit as many of the following characteristics as possible: genuine love for children, warmth, self-discipline, self-sacrifice, respect, patience, enthusiasm, Christian attitude, energy, cleanliness, appropriate dress, godliness, and a desire for excellence. They should be students of the Bible, creative in methods and communication of Scriptures, and able to build rapport and respect that produce proper responses, respectful attitudes, and behavior pleasing unto the Lord.

Realize that you may not find enough people who possess all the characteristics and qualifications for ministry. For those who lack some of these or who don't feel confident to minister, plan opportunities that will provide help. A training seminar for preschool and children's workers will help accomplish this purpose.

ETA has excellent seminar resources to accomplish this training titled *Teaching Preschoolers with Confidence* and *Teaching Children with Confidence.*

A godly couple makes a good team providing both male and female images before the children. A couple can work closely together and be supportive both in planning and prayer. Since the ministry of the children's church leaders is a major one, they should not be expected to handle other major responsibilities in the church.

Children's churches that are divided into more than one age group may need an assistant director for each division. A pianist who is familiar with children's songs and a children's choir director will also be needed for each division. If your church lacks music personnel, good taped music can be used effectively in place of live music.

Program

Helping children to worship is a challenging and profitable ministry. Remember that children, too, can respond to the Bible's admonition that our Heavenly Father is seeking those who will worship Him in spirit and in truth (John 4:23).

Because of this, do not underestimate the children's potential to learn. Stretch them a bit. Establish from the very first that the Bible is God's revelation to people and is without question the ultimate source of truth. Present truth so that they stand in awe of the great and mighty God they are taught to worship. If they are to follow and obey God's Word, the majesty of God, Christ, and the Holy Spirit must be comprehended by simple faith.

An actual formal worship service will generally follow the pattern of the adult service. It will include music, prayer, Scripture, offering, message, choir or special music, with each part adapted to the age level of the group.

Children's church is a worship service for children. Not only must program activities be geared to the age level; but time schedules must also be adjusted. To keep children interested, the program must move along steadily, with carefully selected music which might include the Gloria Patri, doxology, appropriate traditional hymns, testimonial, and joyous songs. Sermons must be interesting and to the point, often in story form and communicated in understandable terminology.

Of course, worship need not be restricted to a formal service. Lois LeBar, in her book, *Children in the Bible School*, reminds us that there is objective and subjective worship, informal and formal worship, spontaneous and unplanned worship, and each of these types has a place in the worship activity of children.

Most children's church programs include learning activities as well. For junior and primary churches these may constitute a separate part of the children's church session. In preschool church the activities are a part of the total program. These include learning new songs which are often visualized, Bible memorization, Bible quizzes, and missions projects. Also, a special time could be set aside for practicing a musical drama to later be presented.

Those churches desiring to use a prepared children's church program should contact their denominational Christian education resources department or their Sunday school curriculum publisher for suggestions and samples.

Children's church offers many opportunities for children to share in the program, an ingredient designed to teach the meaning of church worship. Receiving the offering, serving as ushers, singing in the choir, leading in prayer, and similar activities give the alert children's church director practical opportunities for teaching.

Facilities and equipment

Rooms and equipment should be conducive to quietness and reverence. The room should be light, airy, and remote enough from the sanctuary to prevent the passage of sound to and from the adult service. If the space is a Sunday school assembly area, someone should be appointed to rearrange the room quickly and neatly for children's church. Proper size chairs should also be used. Atmosphere and environment will either make or break the effectiveness of children's worship experiences. An atmosphere of disorganization, uncomfortable temperature, improper seating, dirty, messy, noisy, disorderly conduct are not conducive to worship or learning of any kind. If it isn't done right, don't do it at all. If the worship time is to guide children into God's presence with thanksgiving, appreciation, reverence, praise, joy, communion, reflection, etc., then it will take conscientious hard work, diligence, prayerfulness, modeling, and maintaining an atmosphere and environment that promotes a worship attitude.

Besides piano and songbooks, a worship center with pulpit or table, offering plates, choir robes, ushers' badges, and audio-visual equipment are desirable.

Financing

Expenses for a children's church program might include cost of songbooks, offering trays, weekly bulletins, and choir equipment. Normally, such expenses are included in the church's education budget.

Summary

Children's church is designed to help children have meaningful worship experiences. It is conducted specifically for children and helps them participate in worship activities on the level of their understanding.

Children are usually graded into preschool, primary, and junior churches, following the Sunday school pattern. Programs include worship and other activities, all designed to provide an experience that will bring children into a closer relationship to God.

Review and discussion questions

1. What is the purpose of children's church?
2. How does children's church relate to family worship in the church?
3. What should be the step-by-step advance preparation for starting a children's church?
4. How can music, prayer, Scripture, and stewardship be made worship experiences in children's church?
5. How may children be involved in planning children's church?
6. What age children should attend children's church?
7. How may children's church be related to other church ministries?
8. What is the program of a children's church?
9. What facilities and personnel are needed for children's church?
10. How can children's church affect the daily life of the child?

Application activities

1. Plan a children's church calendar with monthly themes for one year.
2. Develop a complete children's church service for a special day such as Christmas, Easter, or Thanksgiving.
3. Assemble a display of clean, attractive, and appropriate pictures, articles, pamphlets, books, and free samples of published materials dealing with children's church.
4. With clear objectives in mind, organize an observation trip to some nearby, well-organized children's church programs.

MISSION
EDUCATION

11

The local church is instrumental in building mission interest and partnership. Since this vital institution is God's change agent to spread the gospel throughout the world, it is from the local church and its educational ministries that His people are nurtured, encouraged, and SENT. Hence, mission education, which uses the church's educational ministry to teach all age levels beginning with children, must be a vital part of every church's ministry. Mission education involves both knowledge and personal involvement.

What is mission education?
Mission education is a graded approach to the study of mission, using church educational ministries to channel mission information and stimulate personal concern for the spread of the gospel everywhere.

Benefits of mission education

Because it considers itself mission-minded, a church may assume that it is teaching mission in its Sunday school and other educational ministries while, in reality, very little specific teaching is being done. One of the important benefits of an organized program is that it enables the church to carry out specific mission education.

A carefully-planned mission education program makes it possible to take the fullest advantage of every mission opportunity. Speakers, mission conferences (or festivals), and lessons will be part of a total mission program.

Planned use of various age group ministries permits mission teaching to be geared to definite needs. This brings mission to the level of the student's understanding and insures that all information presented is meaningful.

Types of mission education

How the program is organized will depend in part on the size of the church. Regardless of the type of organization, however, one goal will be to involve as many of the church's educational ministries as possible.

Through the mission committee

In most churches a member of the Christian education board may be responsible for mission education. This individual works closely with the church mission committee in planning mission education in the various church educational ministries. In some churches, the mission committee encourages mission education and works closely with the Christian education board in determining what kind of mission education is best suited to each church educational program.

Through age-group leaders or committees

This further extends the use of the mission committee or person on the Christian education board responsible for mission education. Normally those responsible for mission education work with and through the established children, youth, and adult division leaders or committees to coordinate the mission education program.

Through mission conferences or festivals

The annual mission conference or festival offers another means of coordinating mission education. All church members—from preschoolers through older adults—can feel that it is their conference and participate in it. A year-round program of planned teaching and activities should then be related to the conference.

Relationship to other church ministries

A mission education program does not replace the church's established mission planning channels. The regular church mission committee is responsible for planning budgets, speakers, conferences or festivals, and similar details; while those responsible for mission education build upon these plans and use them in an effective mission education ministry.

Coordination of planning is vital. The mission education program is under the board of Christian education and thus related to the total church educational ministry. Often the mission education representative serves with the church mission committee.

Organizing mission education

Personnel, program, facilities, equipment, and finances are important in the organization of church mission education.

Personnel

Regardless of the size or how the church is organized, effective mission education requires dedicated leadership. All individuals with responsibility for mission education need to have a passion for mission and must be organized.

For any mission program to be effective, the whole church needs to be dedicated to spreading the gospel throughout the world. Often church leadership is reluctant to emphasize mission because they are afraid they themselves might become convicted to accept the call to mission. In reality every believer must account to the Lord someday about how well they responded to the Great Commission.

Effective mission education must begin in the home and from there it can be broadened and enriched by local church educational ministries and the pulpit.

In every Christian home, missionary plaques and pictures can be displayed, missionary letters read regularly in family devotions, and visiting missionaries entertained.

The pastor plays an important role in keeping mission at the forefront of the church's programming. His influence always motivates the interests and involvement of the entire congregation.

Usually a *mission education coordinator* is needed. This person is a member of the board of Christian education or church mission committee or both.

In order to provide information and encourage involvement in mission, the coordinator must keep in touch with all the church ministries. He/she will help assign mission speakers and projects to church educational ministries in a coordinated schedule.

Most churches also have a *church mission committee*. This committee is usually made up of a chairperson who directs and promotes the program and works with other church ministries, a librarian who usually works with the church librarian in cataloging and distributing mission materials, and a secretary who keeps mission records. The secretary also corresponds with mission personnel who are currently receiving support from the church.

Program

Whatever the age level of ministry emphasis, mission education can be a focus. The entire congregation needs to be taught that they are in partnership in spreading the gospel throughout the world.

Every believer can be personally involved in mission by intercessory prayer and financial partnership. Even if it is impossible for them to accept a call to go, they can keep mission needs and personnel before the Lord by their daily intercession and financial giving.

Mission education should be part of the *Sunday school* program. The mission education coordinator can help each department with resources and program ideas on such emphases as "the mission field of the month." Many students should be used in these programs, providing personal involvement. Sometimes it helps to direct attention to a certain age person on the mission field. For example, a first-grade class may correspond with and even collect funds to buy gifts for a child of the same age in a missionary family. In this way all the students share the excitement of getting to know and provide for an individual their own age.

Presession activities can also be directed toward mission education. Scrapbooks made for mission hospitals, magazine pictures cut out and mounted for the church library files, murals prepared for the mission conference, skits practiced, prayer requests written out for class use all emphasize the task of world evangelization in a practical way.

Adult Sunday school electives might include a mission education course. This course might present an overview of world mission ministry. (The ETA course, *World Missions Today*, is well suited for this purpose.)

Youth group meetings should regularly include a mission emphasis as well. The mission education coordinator, together with the youth sponsor(s) and the youth leaders, can work out a long-range program as part of the regular youth program planning. The plan should include programs on the meaning and application of witnessing about mission by the youth, study of mission field and problems, contact and interaction with missionaries, and perhaps practical mission experiences. Sometimes these experiences include a trip to a mission work during a vacation period to accomplish a short-term service project.

The mission education coordinator will again correlate all planning with what is being done in the other church education ministries, such as the Sunday school. The emphasis in the youth program will be toward involvement opportunities.

Boys and girls club programs may also do crafts related to mission. Their projects might include making a set of flags of the nations, constructing models of a mission work, or writing letters to foreign and missionary family children who are their same age. Clubs should have opportunity to choose projects and plan how to achieve their goals.

Church mission conferences or festivals should include participation by all age groups and each church educational ministry. One part of the conference may use key leaders of each ministry in the church to report on their particular group's activities.

Adult Sunday school classes, mission societies, and fellowship organizations can be given specific responsibilities such as, giving special reports on the mission fields represented, conducting mission prayer meetings, entertaining visiting missionaries, and preparing displays. Sometimes individual adults or couples have been financially able to visit a mission field to observe the work or even to serve on a short-term basis. These experiences have often helped the entire church to become more mission-minded and enthusiastic for spreading the gospel throughout the world.

The great potential of youth should be used to its fullest. They may be given responsibility for directing a mission service. Challenge them to investigate the fields represented and have a panel ready to interview the mission representative(s). Arrange for youth to usher, provide special music, or present a special mission emphasis on certain nights as well.

A separate children's series of meetings may be conducted at the same time as the adult services. At least two missionaries are needed to alternate in the two services.

With proper adult supervision, children's committees can be arranged so that the children's meetings become a means of training the young for leadership. Committees could include: publicity (e.g. have a poster contest), room arrangements and decorating, program, ushering, prayer meetings, and finances.

Children and adults can share together as families or small groups in working on items such as decorations, displays, and mailing announcements. One night may be designated as Sunday school night when teachers sit with their classes, another could be club night with boys and girls involved in the program.

Facilities and equipment

Mission education can use all of the church's educational equipment. Special mission supplies might include:

Literature, such as mission study books, biographies, novels, magazine articles, and pictures.

Visual resources, such as maps on which name tags can be pinned, globes, pictures for mission stories, videos and/or filmstrips of missionary life and challenges, and flags of all nations.

Audio resources, such as records and tapes about mission works and from missionaries.

In addition, handwork, such as murals, models, puppets, and dioramas will enhance the impact of mission education.

Normally, mission education materials should be located in and issued from the church library or resource center.

Financing

The church budget should include costs of operating the mission education program. When sufficient funds are provided in budget allotments, all offerings received for mission during a conference can be released for direct mission activity. Some churches will budget mission separately, making it necessary to decide whether mission education belongs in the mission or the church education section of the budget.

Summary

Mission education helps a church stimulate personal concern for the spread of the gospel everywhere. This goal is best accomplished through the church's educational ministries, using a graded program of activities and materials.

The key to a successful program is having a local church that has a real passion for mission. The most effective mission education programs have a mission education coordinator, who usually is a member of the Christian education board. Often he/she works with a committee whose major responsibility is to arrange with the various church ministries, such as the Sunday school and youth groups, for involvement in a definite program of mission teaching and experience.

In many churches the climax of mission education is the annual mission conference or festival. This should involve the entire church and have meaning for every age group. The stimulus received from a conference provides motivation for the mission program throughout the year.

Review and discussion questions

1. What is church mission education?
2. How can local church leadership instill a "passion for mission" in their membership?
3. Discuss the implications of the statement, "Mission education is more than just giving facts about a foreign field."
4. Who should be responsible for church mission education?
5. How can the Sunday school participate in mission education?
6. What is the relationship of the mission education organization to the church mission committee?
7. How can youth share in a church mission conference?
8. What organization is needed for developing a church program of mission education?
9. Consider what your church can do to reach the home mission field (your community) in ways not being utilized at present.

Application activities

1. Appoint a committee to investigate and list the materials for mission education now available to your church.
2. Develop a questionnaire on mission education activity to be given to the members of each educational ministry of your church to determine the interest and needs in mission study.
3. Plan at least three things your church might do to improve its mission education program.

Organizations which help

Contact your denominational headquarters, mission agencies whose missionaries your church supports, or one or more of the following interdenominational organizations.

Intercristo
P.O. Box 9323
Seattle, WA 98109

Interdenominational Foreign Mission Association (IFMA)
Box 395
Wheaton, IL 60189-0395

Evangelical Foreign Mission Association (EFMA)
1405 G Street NW
Washington, DC 20005

Association of Church Mission Committees (ACMC)
Box ACMC
Wheaton, IL 60189

BOARD OF CHURCH EDUCATION

12

The ministries presented in this text can become a confusing schedule of unrelated activities as they are put to use in many local churches. Others, however, have learned a key to coordinating their educational programs can be through a church education board or committee.

The biblical ideal of a teaching church calls for organization, administration, and clear statements of policy. Creating and maintaining a board of church education is a practical way to accomplish these volunteer tasks.

Failure to adequately provide for coordination can weaken the entire church ministry. Educational ministries such as the Sunday school and church youth group sometimes tend to operate in isolation. Competition for leadership, finances, and loyalties of people may develop to serious proportion. Judging the success of an endeavor by counting people, their offerings, and such is simply inadequate. If any program is allowed to grow without the design and purpose of growth in Christ through the local church, it will have little basis for evaluation.

What is a board of church education?

A board of church education is a body of church leaders elected or appointed to coordinate and/or advise the church's educational program.

Just as the church assigns responsibility for worship and service, or delegates the management of property and finances, so the teaching program is entrusted to a board of church education. The general purposes of the board are:
- to establish and clarify educational goals
- to unify the educational program
- to evaluate and improve educational outcomes
- to extend the church's educational ministry
- to vitalize its spiritual impact

Benefits of a board of church education

A board becomes a means whereby the church's various educational activities fit into a unified whole. Overlapping of purpose and function are avoided, and the result is a balanced program.

With a board, decisions and programs need not be the responsibility of any one individual. New programs and actions affecting policy and procedures are likely to be accepted by the congregation after a board has conducted a full study and consultation. An active board provides the means for anticipating and fulfilling leadership needs. Education, by its very nature, is a continuous, ongoing ministry and should never be dependent only upon the tenure of persons in charge.

Types of church education boards

Although other structures may be found in churches, most boards are either representative, elected, or a combination of these two types.

Representative

The council type of representative board is composed entirely of people who serve by virtue of their position in the educational program. That is, they represent specific areas, such as the Sunday school or youth program. Those favoring this type of board contend that the people who superintend educational ministries ought to have a direct voice in policy making. Board membership may vary from three or four to as many as nine or ten, depending upon the size of the educational program.

Elected

A second type is the elected board composed entirely of people selected for their broad interest in church education. Those who favor this type of board contend that the major responsibility of setting policy calls for objective leadership. Often those closest to direct leadership are not able to be as objective as others in evaluating their work and reaching decisions affecting the total scope of ministry. The church education board does not act in isolation but thoroughly studies all issues, talks to all concerned, and then makes its decisions.

Combination

A third type of board combines the values of the first two. Many churches create a board composed of individuals elected at large by the church, as well as representative members who serve on the board by virtue of their position. Ideally, this type of board assures a healthy balance between direct representation and church-wide concern. The committee chairperson should exemplify the balance in leadership skills that will emerge from the blending of such committee members.

Relationship to church board and leaders

Often a *church board* (e.g. deacons, elders, executives) directs and coordinates all church activities. Churches with this arrangement may prefer to have the church education board accountable to this leadership board. A close relationship may be achieved by the chairperson (and/or co-chairperson) of the church education board serving on the church board. Or, a member of the church board may regularly attend church education board meetings in an ex officio capacity. The church education board could also make regular reports to the leadership board as well as the congregation.

Other churches divide the responsibility among several boards. In this case, the board of church education has its duties clearly defined, perhaps by the church constitution, and operates accordingly.

The relationship of the board to the *pastor* of the church needs to be clearly defined as well. Usually the pastor is an ex officio member of all boards with voting privileges. That is, he serves on the board by virtue of his office as pastor. He should be welcome at all meetings. When the church staff does not include a minister or director of church education, the pastor takes an active part in guiding the activities of the board.

The board's relationship to a *director of church education* also needs to be established. Depending upon the guidelines of the church's constitution, a director of church education, like the pastor, is an ex officio member of the board, and is responsible for implementing the board's counsel. As an employed staff member of the church, the director of church education works with all the educational programs and their leaders. Generally, for long-range effectiveness it may not be best for the director to serve as chairperson of the board.

The *Sunday school superintendent* also has a vital relationship to the church educational board. Sunday school affairs are a major concern to the group and it may be advisable to have the superintendent serve as an ex officio member of the board, if not already included.

Organizing a church education board

Four basic steps in organizing a new board of church education are:

1. Determine the areas of responsibility for the board in relationship to the official church board and congregation.
2. Determine board size and type of membership, taking into consideration qualifications and method of member selection.
3. Secure church action. This may call for constitutional amendment.
4. Select the members as determined and plan for initial meetings and agendas.

Personnel

Board members are to be elected for a specified time of service. Revolving terms of one to two years will assure board continuity. The pastor or director of church education, Sunday school superintendent, youth director, and other ministry representatives may serve on the board in an ex officio capacity.

Members are to be chosen for their interest in and understanding of the church's educational program.

Much of the responsibility for an effectively functioning board rests with the chairperson. The duties of the chairperson include:

- Arranging and conducting the regular meetings of the board. (Most find it necessary to meet monthly.)
- Appointing any committees that may be needed to fulfill the objectives of the board.
- Preparing an agenda for each meeting in cooperation with the pastor or director of church education.
- Making all necessary reports to the church.
- Supervising the leadership activities of other board members

Duties

The responsibilities of a church education board vary from church to church, but usually include the following:

- The board should periodically make a careful survey of the educational program, facilities, equipment, budget, leadership, and curriculum to discover strengths and weaknesses.
- After reviewing their findings, the board might then recommend changes and improvements.
- The board should assist groups in defining clear-cut objectives and developing programs to meet them. It seeks to keep the entire educational program established on the Word of God.
- The board may approve all curricula for use in the church, after consultation with the educational leadership. Where a published curriculum is unavailable, guidelines should be established for the creative work of teachers and leaders.
- The board seeks to unify staff recruitment, protects church members from becoming overloaded, and giving aid in securing personnel when necessary. Surveying teachers and leaders needed, listing prospective staff members, setting standards for teachers, developing a plan for recruitment, and approving all church education staff members may represent major board duties.
- The board gives high priority to an adequate and continuous program of teacher and leader education. This could include a standard of certification for all teachers and other staff in the church educational ministry.
- The board works closely with the finance committee or board of trustees. It is responsible for the adequate budgeting of funds for its programs.

The board should foster educational awareness and understanding in the congregation as well as utilizing methods such as displays, open houses for parents, and reports to the congregation.

As leaders supervise and administer the work, the board receives regular reports and observes programs in action. It serves as a clearing house for schedules and activities to keep the total educational ministry coordinated.

Dividing responsibilities

Churches usually organize the board membership into functional groups, or subcommittees. One way to structure these subgroups is to divide into age-group interest. Commonly, members are assigned to one of four levels of age interest: preschool, children, youth (teens), or adults. Special areas such as leadership education, mission and stewardship, curriculum, etc. would then be the concern of the entire board upon recommendation of the subcommittee. A sample organization plan appears below.

Another approach might be to divide board members into groupings that concentrate his or her effort in one major area: library, equipment and facilities, family life education, etc. Depending on board size, each area may be represented by a subcommittee or a single person. An organizational plan might look like this:

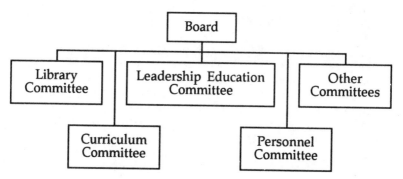

A third organizational pattern simply combines these two plans. Remember that the purpose of delegating responsibility within the board is to develop a functional relationship with all phases of education in the church.

Summary

The board of church education gives unity to the educational ministries of the church. It guards against competition for leadership, finances, and loyalties among the various ministries. It evaluates progress and problems.

Boards may be of the council type which are made up of representatives appointed by each of the church's ministries. Or they may be comprised of members elected directly from the congregation. Many churches use a combination of the two types.

Among the major responsibilities of the board are establishing the church's educational policies and recruiting and training leaders.

Review and discussion questions

1. Why is a board of church education important in the church's ministry?
2. What types of boards are being used?
3. What are the steps to organize a new board?
4. What are the major duties of a church education board?
5. On what basis are board members chosen?
6. Discuss the type of board best suited for your church.
7. What relationship should the pastor or director of church education, and Sunday school superintendent have to the board?
8. How could a board in your church promote educational awareness?

Application activities

1. Write a description of a board and its duties for inclusion in a church constitution.
2. Visit several churches which have boards and reports on how their boards are organized. If possible, attend a meeting of a board of church education and write a summary of the activities.
3. Outline sample agendas for the first three meetings of a board of church education in a newly organized church.

BIBLIOGRAPHY

Chapter 1

Anthony, Michael J. et al. *Foundations of Ministry*. Wheaton, IL: Victor Books, 1992.

Barna, George. *The Frog in the Kettle*. Ventura, CA: Regal Books, 1990.

_____. *How to Find Your Church*. Minneapolis: World Wide Publications, 1989.

_____. *Marketing the Church*. Colorado Springs, CO: NavPress, 1988.

_____. *User Friendly Churches*. Ventura: Regal Books, 1991.

Brown, Carolyn C. *Developing Christian Education in the Smaller Church*. Nashville: Abingdon Press, 1982.

Clark, Robert E.; Johnson, Lin; Sloat, Allyn K. (eds.) *Christian Education: Foundations for the Future*. Chicago: Moody Press, 1991.

Cionca, John R. *Solving Church Education's Ten Toughest Problems*. Wheaton: Victor Books, 1990.

Gangel, Kenneth O. and Hendricks, Howard H. (eds.) *Christian Educators Handbook on Teaching*. Wheaton: Victor Books, 1989.

Plueddemann, James E. Lois E. LeBar's *Education That is Christian*. Wheaton: Victor Books, 1989.

Westing, Harold J. *Multiple Church Staff Handbook*. Grand Rapids, MI: Kregel Publications, 1985.

Chapter 2

Arterburn, S. and Felton, J. *Toxic Faith*. Nashville: Thomas Nelson Publishers, 1991.

Balswick, J.O. and J.K. *The Family*. Grand Rapids: Baker Book House, 1989.

Edge, Findley B. *Teaching for Results*. Nashville: Broadman Press, 1956.

Gangel, Kenneth O. *The Family First*. Winona Lake, IN: Brethren Missionary Herald Books, 1979.

Larson, J. *Growing a Healthy Family*. Minneapolis: Augsburg Publishing House, 1986.

Sell, C. M. *Family Ministry*. Grand Rapids: Zondervan Publishing House, 1981.

Chapter 3

Capehart, Jody. *Becoming a Treasured Teacher.* Wheaton: Victor Books, 1992.

Evangelical Training Association. *The Church at Study.* Wheaton: ETA, 1992.

_____. *Ministering with Confidence* audio cassette series. Wheaton: ETA, 1991.

Friedman, Matt. *The Master Plan of Teaching.* Wheaton: Victor Books, 1990.

Gangel, Kenneth O. *You Can Be An Effective Sunday School Superintendent.* Wheaton: Victor Books, 1981.

Halverson, Delia. *How to Train Volunteer Teachers.* Nashville: Abingdon Press, 1991.

Westing, Harold J. *The Super Superintendent.* Denver: Accent Books, 1980.

Chapter 4

Dibbert, Michael T. and Wichern, Frank B. *Growth Groups: A Key To Christian Fellowship and Spiritual Maturity in the Church.* Grand Rapids: Zondervan Publishing House, 1985.

Hadaway, C. Kirk, Wright, Stuart A., and DuBose, Francis M. *Home Cell Groups and House Churches.* Nashville: Broadman Press, 1987.

Kunz, Marilyn and Schell, Catherine. *How to Start a Bible Study.* Wheaton: Tyndale Publishing House, 1970.

Lum, Ada. *How to Begin an Evangelistic Bible Study.* Downers Grove, IL: InterVarsity Press, 1971.

McBride, Neal F. *How to Lead Small Groups.* Colorado Springs: NavPress, 1990.

Plueddemann, James E. and Carol E. *Pilgrims in Progress.* Wheaton: Harold Shaw, 1990.

Richards, Lawrence O. *Sixty-nine Ways to Start a Study Group and Keep It Growing.* 2nd ed. Grand Rapids: Zondervan Publishing House, 1980.

Chapter 5

Beaty, Willie. *Backyard Bible Club Director's Guide.* Nashville: Convention Press, 1985.

Children's Ministry That Works: The Basics and Beyond. Loveland, CO: Group Books, 1991.

Daniel, Eleanor. *The ABC's of VBS.* Cincinnati: Standard Publishing Co., 1984.

DeVries, Betty and Loeks, Mary. *Bible Activity Sheets for Special Days.* Reproducible. Grand Rapids: Baker Book House, 1987.

DeVries, Nellie. *Easy-to-use Bible Activity Sheets*. Grand Rapids: Baker Book House, 1989.

Erickson, Donna and LaRochelle, David. *Prime Time Together... With Kids: Creative Ideas, Activities, Games, and Projects*. Minneapolis: Augsburg Fortress Publishers, 1992.

Gaither, Gloria and Dobson, Shirley. *Let's Make a Memory*. Irving, TX: Word, Inc., 1983.

Lynn, David and Kathy. *Great Games*. Grand Rapids: Zondervan Publishing House, 1990.

Reaching and Teaching Through VBS. Nashville: Convention Press, 1984.

Self, Margaret (ed.) *Effective Year-round Bible Ministries*. Ventura: Gospel Light, 1981.

Chapter 6

Ball, A. and Ball, B. *Basic Camp Management*. Martinsville, IN: ACA, 1987.

Genne, Elizabeth and William. *Church Family Camps and Conferences*. Valley Forge, PA: Judson Press, 1979.

Mackay, Joy. *Creative Camping*. Wheaton: Victor Books, 1984.

Mattson, Lloyd. *Build Your Church Through Camping*. Duluth, MN: Camping Guideposts, 1984.

Raus, Robert. *Ministry Through Camping*. Nashville: Convention Press, 1990.

Reichter, A. *The Group Retreat Book*. Loveland: Group Books, 1983.

Chapter 7

Cerling, Charles E. *The Divorced Christian*. Grand Rapids: Baker Book House, 1984.

Evangelical Training Association. *Working with Adults*. Wheaton: ETA, 1991.

Fagerstrom, D. (ed.) *Singles Ministry Handbook*. Wheaton: Victor Books, 1988.

Guernsey, Dennis. *A New Design for Family Ministry*. Elgin, IL: David C. Cook Publishing, 1983.

Loth, Paul E. *Teaching Adults with Confidence*. Wheaton: Evangelical Training Association, 1984.

Murray, Dick. *Strengthening the Adult Sunday School Class*. Nashville: Abingdon Press, 1981.

Sell, Charles M. *Transitions Through Adult Life*. Grand Rapids: Zondervan Publishing House, 1991.

Swindoll, Charles R. *Divorce: When It All Comes Tumbling Down*. Portland, OR: Multnomah Productions, 1981.

Wilbert, Warren. *Strategies for Teaching Christian Adults*. Grand Rapids: Baker Book House, 1980.

Chapter 8

Benson, W. S. and Senter, M. H. *The Complete Book of Youth Ministry*. Chicago: Moody Press, 1987.

Burns, R. and Campbell, P. *Create in Me a Youth Ministry*. Wheaton: Victor Books, 1986.

Bynum, Bill. *Teaching Youth with Confidence*. Wheaton: Evangelical Training Association, 1983.

Griffin, Kathryn. *Teaching Teens the Truth*. Nashville: Broadman, 1978.

Ludwig, Glenn E. *Building an Effective Youth Ministry*. Nashville: Abingdon Press, 1979.

Richards, Lawrence O. *Youth Ministry*. Grand Rapids: Zondervan Publishing House, 1985.

Yaconelli, M. and Burns, J. *High School Ministry*. Grand Rapids: Zondervan Publishing House, 1986.

Chapter 10

Drushal, Mary Ellen. *On Tablets of Human Hearts*. Grand Rapids: Zondervan Publishing House, 1991.

Fillmore, Donna. *Leading Children in Worship*. Kansas City: Beacon Hill Press, 1981.

Huttar, Leora. W. *Church Time for Preschoolers*. Denver: Accent Books, 1979.

Smith, Daniel H. *How to Lead a Child to Christ*. Chicago: Moody Press, 1987.

Stewart, Sonja M. and Berryman, Jerome. *Young Children and Worship*. Louisville, KY: Westminster/John Knox Press, 1988.

Sullivan, Jessie P. *Object Lessons and Stories for the Children's Church*. Grand Rapids: Baker Book House, 1979.

Zuck, Roy B. and Clark, Robert E. (eds.) *Childhood Education in the Church*. Chicago: Moody Press, 1986.

Chapter 11

Hulbert, Terry C. and Mulholland, Kenneth B. *World Missions Today*. Wheaton: Evangelical Training Association, 1990.

Kane, J. Herbert. *The Christian World Mission: Today and Tomorrow*. Grand Rapids: Baker Book House, 1981.

_____. *Understanding Christian Missions*. Grand Rapids: Baker Book House, 1986.

Missions Education Handbook. Wheaton: Association of Church Missions Committees, 1985.

Stott, John R. W. *Christian Mission in the Modern World*. Downers Grove, IL: InterVarsity Press, 1976.

Chapter 12

Cionca, J. R. *The Trouble-shooting Guide to Christian Education.* Denver: Accent Books, 1986.

Gangel, K. O. *Building Leaders for Christian Education.* Chicago: Moody Press, 1981.

Gangel, Kenneth O. *So You Want to be a Leader.* Harrisburg, PA: Christian Publications, Inc., 1979.

Getz, Gene A. *Sharpening the Focus of the Church.* Wheaton: Victor Books, 1984.

Kilinski, Kenneth and Wofford, Jerry. *Organization and Leadership in the Local Church.* Grand Rapids: Zondervan Publishing House, 1979.

LeBar, L. E. *Focus on People in Christian Education.* Old Tappan, NJ: Fleming H. Revell, 1968.

Mead, Daniel L. and Allen, Darrell J. *Ministry by Objectives.* Wheaton: Evangelical Training Association, 1978.

Powell, Paul W. *How To Make Your Church Hum.* Nashville: Broadman Press, 1977.

Richards, Lawrence O. *Christian Education.* Grand Rapids: Zondervan Publishing House, 1988.

Schaller, Lyle E. *Effective Church Planning.* Nashville: Abingdon Press, 1979.

Senter, M. *Recruiting Volunteers in the Church.* Wheaton: Victor Books, 1990.

Wilhoit, Jim. *Christian Education and the Search for Meaning.* 2nd ed. Grand Rapids: Baker Book House, 1991.